UNDERSTANDING
REGRESSION ANALYSIS

Second Edition

Quantitative Applications in the Social Sciences

A SAGE PUBLICATIONS SERIES

Quantitative Applications in the Social Sciences

A SAGE PUBLICATIONS SERIES

To our children,

Leanne

Nathan

Meghan

Jennifer

David

SAGE was founded in 1965 by Sara Miller McCune to support the dissemination of usable knowledge by publishing innovative and high-quality research and teaching content. Today, we publish over 900 journals, including those of more than 400 learned societies, more than 800 new books per year, and a growing range of library products including archives, data, case studies, reports, and video. SAGE remains majority-owned by our founder, and after Sara's lifetime will become owned by a charitable trust that secures our continued independence.

Los Angeles | London | New Delhi | Singapore | Washington DC | Melbourne

UNDERSTANDING REGRESSION ANALYSIS

An Introductory Guide

Second Edition

Larry D. Schroeder
Syracuse University

David L. Sjoquist
Georgia State University

Paula E. Stephan
Georgia State University

Los Angeles | London | New Delhi
Singapore | Washington DC | Melbourne

FOR INFORMATION:

SAGE Publications, Inc.
2455 Teller Road
Thousand Oaks, California 91320
E-mail: order@sagepub.com

SAGE Publications Ltd.
1 Oliver's Yard
55 City Road
London, EC1Y 1SP
United Kingdom

SAGE Publications India Pvt. Ltd.
B 1/I 1 Mohan Cooperative Industrial Area
Mathura Road, New Delhi 110 044
India

SAGE Publications Asia-Pacific Pte. Ltd.
3 Church Street
#10-04 Samsung Hub
Singapore 049483

Copyright © 2017 by SAGE Publications, Inc.

Printed in the United States of America

ISBN 978-1-5063-3288-8

This book is printed on acid-free paper.

Acquisitions Editor: Helen Salmon
Editorial Assistant: Chelsea Pearson
Production Editor: Kelly DeRosa
Copy Editor: Cate Huisman
Typesetter: C&M Digitals (P) Ltd.
Proofreader: Jennifer Grubba
Indexer: Will Ragsdale
Cover Designer: Candice Harman
Marketing Manager: Susannah Goldes

SFI Certified Sourcing
www.sfiprogram.org
SFI-00453

16 17 18 19 20 10 9 8 7 6 5 4 3 2 1

CONTENTS

SERIES EDITOR'S INTRODUCTION

Regression analysis is the "bread and butter" of social science research. A scan of the *American Economic Review*, *American Political Science Review*, *American Sociological Review*, and *American Educational Research Journal* shows that at least half of the articles published in the most recent issue of these flagship journals involve regression analysis. The same can be said about many journals in these fields. Social science research, as well as research in many other fields, including business, law and public policy, is largely inaccessible without at least some working knowledge of regression analysis, the logic that underlies it, and the basics of interpretation. For readers new to regression, it is difficult to know where to start: applications motivate interest in the statistics; yet without some working knowledge of the statistics, it is difficult to understand and appreciate the applications.

Understanding Regression Analysis: An Introductory Guide, Second Edition provides an accessible, easy-to-read, and non-technical introduction to multiple regression analysis. It is appropriate for upper-division undergraduate and introductory graduate courses needing a concise but thorough coverage of linear regression. Because of its emphasis on application, graduate students will find it a useful resource as they are mastering the technical details of regression. Trained researchers wanting a quick refresher on the core ideas of regression will also benefit from this volume. It is short, well-organized, and for those with prior familiarity with regression, can be read in an evening.

Understanding Regression Analysis covers what is needed to understand applications of regression analysis. It begins with a clear exposition of a linear relationship and linear regression, then proceeds to multiple regression, hypothesis testing, and extensions. It concludes with problems and issues associated with linear regression. The authors cover an impressive number of topics: least squares regression; correlation and regression coefficients; sampling; goodness of fit; standard deviations, hypothesis testing, Type

I and Type II error; standard errors; statistical significance; Student's t distribution; right-, left- and two-tail tests; confidence intervals; cross-sectional, longitudinal, and panel data; micro and aggregate data; dummy variables; and interactions. The final chapter of the volume touches on the kinds of issues that may arise in actual application and the ways analysts typically respond. It discusses in a pragmatic and accessible way some of the problems associated with omitting a relevant variable, including an irrelevant variable, incorrectly specifying functional form, measurement error, selection bias, multicollinearity, autocorrelation, heteroscedasticity, and endogeneity. In doing so, it briefly introduces more advanced topics such as fixed effects models, interactions, time series analysis, simultaneous equations, regression discontinuity designs, instrumental variables, and limited dependent variables. With grounding in the basics, readers can understand key results from these more sophisticated analyses, even if they are not in a position to undertake these analyses themselves.

The first edition of *Understanding Regression Analysis*, published thirty years ago, remains one of the most popular "little green covers" in the QASS series. The second edition retains all of the strengths of the first: it is well-organized, concise, and thorough. The authors have also made improvements. They have updated symbols and terminology to correspond with current usage. They include an appendix showing what regression output looks like from four different statistical software packages (SAS, Stata, SPSS, R) and also from the Excel spreadsheet program. Importantly, the second edition of *Understanding Regression Analysis* draws a wide array of examples from the current literature, selecting ones that will appeal to a broad audience. These include the relative position of states in educational performance, the impact of the great recession on volunteering, gender-based discrimination and maternity leave policies, the impact of winning the Nobel Prize on the number of times a scientist's work is cited, the effect of copyright laws on the composition of new operas, the effects of immigration attitudes on political party identification, and the impact of the great recession on lightweight vehicle sales, among others. The examples include different levels of measurement in explanatory variables, from nominal to ratio. They illustrate diverse units of analysis, from individuals to states to countries. They also demonstrate the use of both cross-sectional and times series data and some of the issues that arise in the analysis of each. In short, the authors pair interesting examples with clear explanations of critical concepts and issues, making the volume accessible to readers at all levels from a broad range of social science disciplines. I am pleased to see an already successful monograph made even better.

Barbara Entwisle
Series Editor

PREFACE

The revised version provides, as did the first edition of this volume, a short, nontechnical explanation of linear regression analysis. We illustrate how regression coefficients are estimated, how they are interpreted, and how they are used in a variety of settings within the social sciences, business, law, and public policy. The techniques used to test hypotheses about the regression coefficients and what the test results do and do not mean are explained. The book also discusses how linear regression techniques can be applied to a variety of different types of data, including data that represent specific groups or time periods, and also how forecasters can use regression analysis to make predictions. Finally, we acknowledge and explain some of the limitations to linear regression analysis.

Our intent is to provide a non-technical understanding of regression analysis, its meaning, and uses. The book is not intended to be a substitute for a course in elementary or applied statistics; however, students enrolled in such courses may find it a useful supplement to their regular textbook. Students in undergraduate or graduate courses that rely on articles that use regression techniques may find this volume useful in interpreting the reported results. Likewise, those who previously took a course or two in statistics may find the book to be a good review of the basic concepts they studied.

Readers of the previous edition of our Sage "Green Book" will find this edition to be equally understandable and accessible. As with the first edition, we assume the reader has no background in statistics and only a limited background in mathematics. The second edition was edited to make the discussion even clearer and to provide improved explanations of various concepts. Boxes were added to highlight basic concepts and to augment text material. All examples are new and are taken from current books and articles. The examples, as well as the discussion in the chapters, also have been broadened substantially to encompass additional areas of the social sciences, business, law, and public policy. We have made the discussion of hypothesis testing in Chapter 3 more in line with the current approaches.

The final two chapters were significantly revised to reflect changes in the approaches to and applications of regression analysis that have become more common since the publication of our first edition.

ACKNOWLEDGMENTS

We are grateful to the late Theodore C. Boyden for providing the encouragement to first undertake this project. Special thanks go to Louis Ederington and Meghan O'Leary who read a draft of the manuscript and provided numerous helpful suggestions. We want to thank Lakshmi Pandey and Laura Wheeler for their assistance, and the great team at SAGE: series editor Barbara Entwisle, project editor Kelly DeRosa, copy editor Cate Huisman, and proofreader Jennifer Grubba. We particularly want to thank our editor Helen Salmon for her support. We also want to acknowledge Cynthia M. Cready, University of North Texas; Andrea Hetling, Rutgers University–New Brunswick; and Kelly D. Strawn, Willamette University who reviewed the previous edition and provided an extensive list of suggestions for improvement. Appreciation is also extended to Wyatt Brown, Marshall University; Elizabeth J. Kiel, Miami University; Grigoris Argeros, Eastern Michigan University; Andrea Hetling, Rutgers University–New Brunswick; David Ansong, University of North Carolina at Chapel Hill; Ross E. Burkhart, Boise State University; Ting Jiang, Metropolitan State University of Denver; Adam Mayer, Colorado State University; and John Stuart Batchelder, University of North Georgia who provided feedback on the second edition manuscript.

ABOUT THE AUTHORS

Larry D. Schroeder is professor emeritus of public administration and international affairs in the Maxwell School, Syracuse University. He holds a PhD from the University of Wisconsin and taught quantitative methods courses at the Maxwell School as well as at Georgia State University and Indiana University. His substantive areas of interest are in public finance and policy, particularly state and local government finance and administration. His research has focused primarily on fiscal decentralization, intergovernmental fiscal relations, and the effects of institutional arrangements on the provision of public services.

David L. Sjoquist is professor of economics in the Andrew Young School of Policy Studies at Georgia State University. He holds a PhD in economics from the University of Minnesota and has taught microeconomic theory, public economics, and statistics. His primary research interests are in state and local public economics, urban economics, and economics of education.

Paula E. Stephan is professor of economics at the Andrew Young School of Policy Studies at Georgia State University and a research associate at the National Bureau of Economic Research. She holds a PhD from the University of Michigan. Her research focuses on the careers of scientists and engineers and the process by which knowledge moves across institutional boundaries in the economy. She has authored or coauthored two additional books and edited three. She has held visiting positions at Harvard University, Cambridge, Massachusetts; Katholieke Universiteit Leuvin, Belgium; the Wissenschaftszentrum für Social Forschung, Berlin, Germany; and the University of Turin, Italy.

Is one's perception of instructors' commitment to diversity influenced by ethnicity?

CHAPTER 1. LINEAR REGRESSION

Introduction

It is likely that you have thought about a variety of relationships between different variables. For example, on a personal level you might have wondered whether studying an additional hour will lead to a substantially better score on an upcoming exam. Or, will getting additional experience in a nonpaid internship increase the likelihood of obtaining a full-time position in an organization you wish to work for. Or, if you go to the gym an additional hour each week, will this lead to a substantial weight loss.

Relationships between variables are also at the heart of many academic disciplines. Political scientists may focus on the possible link between contributions to political leaders and decisions those leaders subsequently take. Economists may be interested in how mortgage interest rates affect the housing market. Marketing firms are likely interested in how different forms of advertising lead to improved sales of a product. Policy analysts are often interested in how a change in a policy, such as a new curriculum in elementary education, might lead to different outcomes, such as improved test scores. Public health researchers might be interested in determining how the incidence of cancer is related to the amount of red meat that is consumed. Others might be interested in how student standardized test scores are related to the marital status, education, and income of the parents, or how wages in metropolitan areas are related to the number of immigrants in the metropolitan area.

The point is that interest in understanding relationships is common and widespread. Researchers, both in the natural and social sciences, often want to delve much more deeply into the nature of those possible relationships. And when the variables of interest, such as contributions to political office seekers and votes on a particular issue, can be quantified, a very common method used for analyzing those relationships is linear regression analysis. Regression analysis is a statistical technique that provides a way of conveniently summarizing the relationship between a variable of interest and one or more variables that are anticipated to influence that variable.

This volume is about linear regression analysis, that is, analysis of cases in which the relationship between the variable to be explained and the other variable or variables can be summarized by a straight line. The volume is intended to provide the reader with a basic understanding of how regression analysis can be carried out, how the results from such analysis are interpreted, and the variety of ways in which regression analysis is used both in academic settings and in public and business arenas. The current chapter illustrates how a single variable can be used to explain variations in another variable, for example, the influence of mortgage interest rates on the number of new houses constructed. Chapter 2 shows how more complex relationships, in which a single variable is hypothesized to depend on two or more variables, can be estimated using regression analysis. For example, how do volume of traffic, speed, and weather conditions affect the number of accidents on highways? In most applications of regression analysis, researchers rely on data that constitute a sample drawn from a population. As is shown in Chapter 3, in these instances it is necessary to test hypotheses in order to generalize the findings to the population from which the sample was drawn. The final two chapters expand on the discussion of regression analysis. Chapter 4 focuses on the data used and Chapter 5 on a variety of problems and issues researchers face when using this technique. Throughout the volume we keep the discussion as simple as possible and provide examples to illustrate how regression analysis is applied in a variety of disciplines. Our objective is to give the reader a solid but basic understanding of linear regression analysis, not to make the reader an expert. Thus many more complex statistical issues are not covered in this book. Readers who wish a more in-depth coverage are referred to the suggested readings provided in Appendix D.

Hypothesized Relationships

The two statements, "The more a political candidate spends on advertising, the larger the percentage of the vote the candidate will receive" and "Mary is taller than Jane," express different types of relationships. The first statement implies that the percentage of the vote that a candidate receives is a function of, or is caused by, the amount of advertising, while in the second statement, no causality is implied. More precisely, the former expresses a *causal* or *functional* relationship while the latter does not. A functional relationship is a statement (often expressed in the form of an equation) of how one variable, called the *dependent* variable, depends on one or more other variables, called *independent* or *explanatory* variables.[1] In the example, the share of the vote a candidate receives is dependent on (is a function of) the amount spent on advertising. Another independent variable that might be included in the analysis is the number of prior years in office, in which case the functional relationship would be stated as, "The candidate's share of the vote depends on the amount of advertising as well as the candidate's prior years in office."

---

[1]Other names used for the dependent variable are left-hand-side variable, regressand, response variable, and endogenous variable. Other names for the independent variable are right-hand-side variable, regressor, stimulus variable, and exogenous variable.

Researchers are often interested in testing the validity or falsity of hypothesized functional relationships, called *hypotheses*[2] or *theories*. We show in Chapter 3 how linear regression is used to test such hypotheses. But first we explain how a regression equation is estimated.

Linear regression analysis is applicable to a vast array of subject matter. Consider the following situations in which regression analysis has been employed: a study of the effect of polluting industries on mortality rates in Chinese cities (Hanlon and Tian 2015), a study of how proximity to fast-food restaurants relates to the percentage of ninth graders who are obese (Currie, Della Vigne, Moretti, and Pathania 2010), a study of the relationship between income tax rebates and sales of hybrid electric vehicles (Chandra, Gulati, and Kandikar 2010), a study of the effect of changes in cigarette prices on smoking among smokers of different smoking intensities (Cavazos-Rehg et al. 2014), and a study showing the effect of severe drops in temperature on the number of trials for the crime of witchcraft in 16th and 17th century Europe (Oster 2004). All of these examples are cases in which the application of regression analysis was useful, although the application was not always as straightforward as the example to which we now turn.

A Numerical Example

To facilitate the discussion of linear regression analysis, the following food consumption example will be referred to throughout the book. Suppose one were asked to investigate by how much a typical family's food expenditure increases as a result of an increase in its income. While most would agree that there is a relationship between income and the amount spent on food, the example is in fact an investigation of an economic theory. The theory suggests that the expenditure on food is a function of family income;[3] that is, $C = f(I)$, read "C is a function of I," where C (the dependent variable) refers to the expenditure on food, and I (the independent variable, sometimes called the regressor) denotes income. Throughout the book we will refer to the theory that C increases as I increases as the hypothesis.[4]

The investigation of the relationship between C and I allows for both testing the theory that C increases as a result of increases in I and obtaining an

---

[2]Hypotheses need not be functional relationships, since it can be hypothesized that Mary is taller than Jane without implying that Mary's height is a function of Jane's height. However, the hypotheses that we discuss are statements of functional relationships.

[3]Economic theory states that the consumption of a product is a function of income, the price of the product, the prices of related products, and the tastes of the consumer. When everything except income is held constant, changes in the consumption of the product become a function of changes in income alone.

[4]Although we use C and I for this example, it is common to refer to the dependent variable as y and the independent variable as x.

estimate of how much food consumption changes as income changes. One can therefore consider the investigation as an analysis of two related questions: (1) Does spending on food increase when a family's income increases? (2) By how much does spending on food change when income increases or decreases? In this chapter we explain how a linear relationship between the two variables is estimated in order to provide descriptive answers to these questions, although, as will be seen in Chapter 3, these questions cannot be answered with certainty.

A common strategy for answering questions such as these is to observe income and food consumption differences among a number of families and note how differences in food consumption are related to differences in income. Here we employ the hypothetical data given in columns 1 and 2 of Table 1.1 to answer this question. The data represent annual income and food consumption information from a sample of 50 families in the United States for one year. Assume that this sample was chosen randomly from the population of all families in the United States.[5] The associated levels of these two variables have been plotted as the 50 points in Figure 1.1. We are

Table 1.1 Food Consumption, Family Income, Family Size, and Gardening Data

(1) Food Consumption	(2) Income	(3) Family Size	(4) Has a Garden
$780	$24,000	1	NO
1,612	20,000	1	NO
1,621	37,436	1	NO
1,820	36,600	2	YES
2,444	10,164	1	YES
3,120	2,500	1	NO
3,952	29,000	1	YES
4,056	40,000	1	NO
4,160	30,154	1	NO
4,160	34,000	1	YES
4,300	46,868	1	NO
4,420	15,000	1	NO
5,200	36,400	2	YES
5,200	25,214	2	YES

[5]In its use in statistics, the term *population* refers to a collection of entities such as firms, states, children, movies, etc. If we were interested in the advertising expenditures of firms, we would draw a sample from the population of all firms.

(1) Food Consumption	(2) Income	(3) Family Size	(4) Has a Garden
6,100	21,400	2	YES
6,240	68,620	2	YES
6,587	1,200	3	NO
7,020	40,000	2	NO
7,040	52,000	1	NO
7,540	31,100	2	NO
7,600	107,602	4	NO
8,060	134,000	2	NO
8,632	59,800	3	NO
8,800	68,000	4	NO
8,812	80,210	2	NO
8,840	67,000	1	NO
9,100	50,000	6	NO
9,150	53,420	1	NO
9,360	55,000	1	NO
9,658	65,000	1	NO
9,660	66,000	2	YES
9,880	28,912	3	YES
10,192	100,000	1	YES
10,296	50,356	4	YES
10,400	45,000	4	NO
11,263	168,000	4	NO
11,700	110,200	4	NO
11,960	75,000	3	NO
12,036	150,200	1	YES
12,064	44,746	2	NO
12,240	171,170	2	NO
12,652	170,000	5	NO
13,260	27,000	2	NO
14,377	132,543	2	YES
14,731	192,220	2	NO
15,300	141,323	4	NO
16,584	84,059	2	NO
16,870	176,915	5	NO
18,776	189,654	5	NO
20,132	151,100	3	NO

Source: Hypothetical data

Figure 1.1 Scatter Diagram of Family Income and Food Consumption

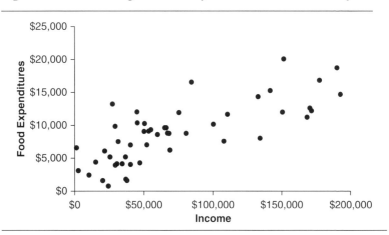

going to use this sample to draw inferences about how income affects food consumption for the population of families.

Casual observation of the points in Figure 1.1 suggests that C increases as I increases. However, the magnitude by which C increases as I increases for the 50 families is not obvious. For this reason the presentation of data in tabular or graphical form is not by itself a particularly useful format from which to draw inferences. These formats are even less desirable as the number of observations and variables increases. Thus we seek a means of summarizing or organizing the data in a more useful manner.

Any functional relationship can conveniently be expressed as a mathematical equation. If one can determine the equation for the relationship between C and I, one can use this equation as a means of summarizing the data. Since an equation is defined by its form and the values of its parameters, the investigation of the relationship between C and I entails learning something from the data about the form and parameters of the equation.

The economic theory that suggests that C is a function of I does not indicate the form of the relationship between C and I. That is, it is not known whether the equation is of a linear or some other, more complex form.[6] In some problems the general form of the equation is suggested by the theory, but since this is not so in the food expenditure problem, it is necessary to specify a particular form. We shall assume that the form of the equation for our problem is that of a straight line, which is the simplest and most

---

[6]As discussed in Chapter 4, there are many different functional forms for an equation relating two variables. For our purposes here, we restrict ourselves to a simple linear function.

commonly used functional form.[7] (A review of the algebraic expression for a straight line is given in Box 1.1.)

Box 1.1 Algebraic Expression for a Straight Line

As you may remember from algebra, a straight line relating two variables X and Y, with Y considered a function of X, can be expressed using the formula $Y = a + bX$, where a and b are numbers; a is the intercept, which is the value of Y when X is zero, and b is the slope, which measures the change in Y associated with a unit increase or decrease in X. For example if $Y = 2.5 + 0.7X$, a two-dimensional graph with Y on the vertical axis and X on the horizontal axis would show the line passing through the vertical axis at $Y = 2.5$ (since X is zero at that point) and with a slope of 0.7, which means that for any one-unit increase in X there is a 0.7-unit increase in Y.

Given this assumption, one can express the functional relationship that exists between C and I for all U.S. families as

$$C = \alpha + \beta I \qquad [1.1]$$

where α (the Greek letter alpha) and β (the Greek letter beta) are the unknown parameters assumed to hold for the population of US families, and are referred to as the *population parameters*.

Given the assumption that the form of the equation of the possible relationship between C and I can be represented by a straight line, what remains is to estimate the values of the population parameters of the equation using our sample of 50 families. The two questions posed earlier refer to the value of the slope—that is, the value of β. The first question asks whether β is greater than zero, while the second asks the value of β. By obtaining an estimate of the value of β, a statement can be made as to the effect of changes in income on the amount spent on food for the 50 families in our sample. As shown in Chapter 3, inferences can be drawn from this estimate of β about the behavior of all families in the population.

Before proceeding, it is important to note the following. The actual or "true" form of the relationship between I and C is not known. We have simply assumed a particular form for the relationship in order to summarize the data

---

[7]Because problems may arise when one specifies a particular functional form when a different form should have been specified, care must be taken in selecting the particular form used. Further, linearity may imply more than just a straight line. These topics are discussed in Chapters 4 and 5.

in Figure 1.1. Further, we do not know the values of the population parameters of the assumed linear relationship between C and I. The task is to obtain estimates of the values of α and β. We will denote these estimates as a and b.[8]

Estimating a Linear Relationship

The question that may come to mind at this point is, "How can it be stated that income and food consumption are related by a precise linear equation when the data points in Figure 1.1 clearly do not lie on a straight line?" The answer comprises three parts. First, the assumption that a straight line is a good summary of the data points does not imply that C and I are related in precisely this manner for every family. Second, the hypothesis is based on the implicit assumption that only income and food consumption differ between these families. However, other things, such as family size and tastes, are not likely to be the same for all families and thus affect the amount spent on food. Third, there is randomness in people's behavior; that is, an individual or family, for no apparent reason, may buy more or less food than some other family that appears to be in exactly the same situation with regard to income, taste, and the like. Thus one would not expect the data points to lie consistently on a straight line even if the line did represent the average response to changes in income.

More formally the regression equation is expressed as

$$C_i = \alpha + \beta I_i + \varepsilon_i \qquad [1.2]$$

In this form we say that food consumption of the *ith* family, C_i, depends on its income, I_i. The term ε_i is referred to as the *error term*, and captures the fact that given the values of α and β, the equation will not exactly predict a family's food consumption given its income for reasons discussed in the previous paragraph.

As noted previously, from the data points in Figure 1.1 it is not obvious how much C increases as I increases; that is, it is uncertain what the slope of the line summarizing the data points should be. To see this, consider the two solid lines that have been arbitrarily drawn through the points in Figure 1.2. Line 1 has the equation $C = 5000 + 0.04I$, and line 2 has the equation $C = 2000 + 0.15I$. Which of these two lines is the better estimate of how food consumption changes as income changes? This is the same as asking which of the two equations is better at summarizing the relationship between C and I found in Table 1.1. More generally, which line among all the straight lines that it is possible to draw through the points in Figure 1.2

---

[8]Note that some authors denote the estimates as $\hat{\alpha}$ and $\hat{\beta}$.

is the "best" in terms of summarizing the relationship between C and I? Regression analysis, in essence, provides a procedure for determining the *regression line*, which is the best straight line (or linear) approximation of the relationship between C and I. This procedure is equivalent to finding particular values for the slope and intercept.

An intuitive idea of what is meant by the process of finding a linear approximation of the relationship between the independent and dependent variables can be obtained by taking a string or ruler and trying to "fit" the points in Figure 1.1 to a line. Move the string up or down, or rotate it until it takes on the general tendency of the points in the graph.

What property should this best-fitting line possess? If asked to select which of the two solid lines in Figure 1.2 is better at summarizing (estimating) the relationship between income and food consumption, one would undoubtedly choose line l, because it is "closer" to the points than line 2. (This is not to imply that line l is the regression line.)

Closeness or distance can be measured in different ways. Two possible measures are the vertical distance and the horizontal distance between the observed points and a line. In the normal case, where the dependent variable is plotted along the vertical axis, distance is measured vertically as the differences between the observed points and a fitted line. This is shown in Figure 1.2, where the vertical dotted line drawn from the data point to line l measures the distance between the observed data point and the line. In this case distance is measured in dollars of consumption, not in feet or inches.

Figure 1.2   Two Possible Summaries of the Income-Consumption Relationship

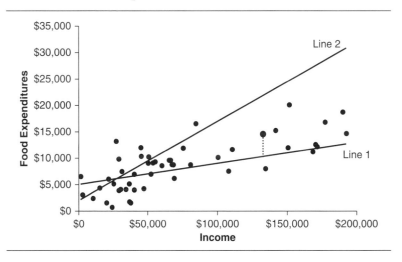

The choice of the vertical distance stems from the theory stating that the value of C depends on the value of I. Thus, for a particular value of income, it is desired that the regression line be chosen so as to predict a value of food consumption that is as close as possible to the value of food consumption observed at that income level.

The regression line cannot minimize the distance for all points simultaneously. In Figure 1.2 it can be seen that some points are closer to line 1, while others are closer to line 2. Thus a method of averaging or summing up all these distances is needed to obtain the best fitting line.

Although several methods exist for summing these distances, the most common method in regression analysis is to find the sum of the squared values of the vertical distances. This is expressed as

$$\sum_{i=1}^{n} (C_i - \hat{C}_i)^2 \qquad [1.3]$$

where C_i is the actual value of C for the ith family, $\hat{C}_i$ (read "C hat sub i") is the value of C for the *ith* family that would be estimated by the regression line and n is the number of observations over which the expression is summed.[9]

Least Squares Regression

In the most common form of regression analysis, the line that is chosen is the one that minimizes

$$\sum_{i=1}^{n} (C_i - \hat{C}_i)^2 \qquad [1.4]$$

which is called the *sum of the squared errors*, frequently denoted *SSE*.[10] For each observation, the distance between the observed and the predicted level of consumption can be thought of as an error, since the observed level of consumption is not likely to be predicted exactly but is missed by some amount $(C_i - \hat{C}_i)$. As noted above, this error may be due, for example, to randomness in behavior or other factors such as differences in family size. Because the squares of the errors are minimized, the term *least squares*

---

[9]If we used the regression equation and calculated the value of consumption for income equal to I_i, the estimated level of consumption would be denoted by $\hat{C}_i$. The symbol Σ (the Greek letter sigma) is the standard symbol for summation. For example, $\sum_{i=1}^{n} C_i$ means to sum the first three values of C (from Table 1.1); that is, $\sum_{i=1}^{3} C_i = \$780 + \$1,612 + \$1,621 = \$4,013$.

[10]Although other estimation methods exist, the focus of this book is least squares regression.

regression analysis is used, with the estimation technique commonly referred to as *ordinary least squares* (OLS).

The reasons for selecting the sum of the squared errors lie in statistical theory that is beyond the scope of this book. However, an intuitive rationale for its selection can be presented. If the errors were not squared, distances above the line would be canceled by distances below the line. Thus it would be possible to have several lines, all of which minimized the sum of the nonsquared errors.[11] It is implicit that closeness is good, while remoteness is bad. It can also be argued that the undesirability of remoteness increases more than in proportion to the error. Thus, for example, an error of four dollars is considered more than twice as bad as an error of two dollars. One way of taking this into account is to weight larger errors more than smaller errors, so that in the process of minimizing it is more important to reduce larger errors. Squaring errors is one means of weighting them.

Let a and b represent the estimated values of α and β for the still unknown regression line. $\hat{C}_i$ can be expressed as $\hat{C}_i = a + bI_i$. Substituting $a + bI_i$ for $\hat{C}_i$ in expression 1.4, the expression for SSE can be rewritten as

$$SSE = \sum_{i=1}^{n} \left(C_i - a - bI_i \right)^2 \qquad [1.5]$$

Note that the term in parentheses in equation 1.5 is the error term, that is, an estimate of ε_i, from equation 1.2.

Expressions for a and b can be found that minimize the value of equation 1.5 and hence give the least squares estimates of α and β, which in turn define the regression line. (See Appendix A for the derivation of the formulas using the calculus.)

For the given set of data in Table 1, the a and b that minimize equation 1.5 are $a = 4{,}155.21$ and $b = +0.064$. (Statistical packages, which are readily available, generate the values of a and b. For purposes of completeness, Appendix A shows how the actual values of a and b are calculated.) Therefore, the least squares line, which is drawn in Figure 1.3, has the equation

$$C = 4{,}155.21 + 0.064I \qquad [1.6]$$

These results mean, for example, that the estimate of consumption for a family whose annual income is \$10,000 is \$4,795.21—that is, \$4,795.21

---

[11]To see this, consider a sample with three observations: $C = 1$, $I = 1$; $C = 2$, $I = 2$; $C = 3$, $I = 3$. Plot the three observations and draw a line through all three points. Now draw a different straight line which passes through the second observation but not the first and third. For both lines, the sum of the nonsquared distances is zero. But note that not all lines that could be drawn would result in a sum of the nonsquared distance being zero, for example, a line drawn through the first observation.

12

Figure 1.3 "Best Fitting" Regression Line

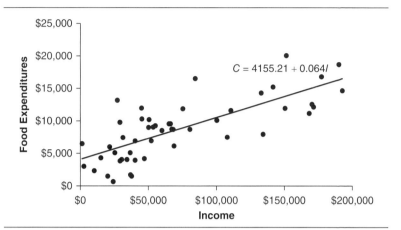

= \$4,155.21 + 0.064(\$10,000). Remember, this is an estimate of C and not necessarily the amount one would observe for a specific family with an income of \$10,000. The value of a, \$4,155.21, is the estimated food consumption for a family with zero income. The value of b, 0.064, implies that for this sample, each dollar change in family income results in a change of \$0.064 in food consumption in the same direction (note the positive sign for b). When interpreting the results of a regression analysis, it is important to keep in mind the unit of measure for the variables used in the equation (see Box 1.2).

Box 1.2 Importance of the Units of Measure

The estimate of the slope coefficient β is interpreted as the change in the dependent variable associated with a one-unit change in the independent variable. In our food example, both income and the amount spent on food are measured in dollars, so a one-unit change is one dollar. But what if each variable had been measured in thousands of dollars? In that case, observations for the first family in Table 1.1 would be 0.780 (thousands of dollars spent on food) and 24 (thousands of dollars income), and the regression result would be $C = 4.15521 + 0.064I$. Here the intercept represents the same 4.15521 thousands of dollars and for each thousand-dollar increase in income (a one-unit increase) there would be an associated 0.064 thousand (in other words, \$64) increase in food consumption. This of course is a 6.4 cent increase in food consumption per dollar increase in income.

But what if income were measured in thousands while C continued to be shown in dollars? Then the resulting equation would be $C = 4155.21 + 64I$. Again this would mean that for each additional one thousand dollars in income (i.e., a one-unit increase in I), there would be an associated \$64 increase in food consumption. The "story" about the relationship between C and I remains the same in spite of the different sizes of the coefficients. The important lesson to keep in mind is to be aware of the units of measure any time you interpret linear regression results.

These conclusions, of course, hold only for this particular sample. When the least squared technique is applied to additional samples of consumers, one would obtain additional (generally different) estimates of α and β.

It is important to point out that regression analysis does not prove causation. Our estimate of β is consistent with the theory that an increase in income causes an increase in food consumption. However, it does not prove causation. Note that we could have reversed the equation, making I depend on C, and argued that higher food consumption makes for healthier and more productive workers who thus have higher incomes. Since I and C increase together, this alternative relationship would also be supported. It would take some alternative experiment or test to determine the direction of the causation. Our estimate of β, however, is not consistent with the theory that food consumption decreases with increases in income.[12]

Note that linear regression requires that the regression equation relating the dependent and independent variables be linear, that is, a straight line. However, the equation relating Y and X does not have to be linear, so long as the estimated regression equation is linear. For example, suppose that we believe that the relationship between Y and X is given by $Y^2 = \alpha + \beta X^2$. Thus, Y and X are not related by a straight line, but the relationship between the variables Y^2 and X^2 is linear, so one can estimate a linear regression using Y^2 and X^2. We return to this topic in Chapter 4.

Examples

Before proceeding, three examples are presented to illustrate how regression analysis is used. Note that these examples have been selected in order to give the reader some idea of the variety of ways in which linear regression has

---

[12]This statement anticipates the discussion of hypothesis testing in Chapter 3. We also show there that the statement depends on more than the sign of the estimated parameter.

14

been utilized in published research. They also represent only a portion of more extensive research that is included in the original articles; reading the entire article will provide much more information on the research that was conducted.

Example 1.1—Change in Education Performance

Goldin and Katz (2008, 346) examine the rise in education levels in the United States during the 20th century and its relationship to economic development. As part of their analysis, they explore how increased educational performance during the last two-thirds of the 20th century differed across states. In particular, they ask if states that had relatively low high school graduation rates in 1938 also had relatively low educational performance levels at the end of the century. To explore this question, they estimated a regression in which the independent variable is the state's high school graduation rate in 1938 and the dependent variable is an index of educational performance for the 1990s. The index averages several National Assessment of Education Progress (NAEP) scores, Scholastic Aptitude Test (SAT) scores, and a measure of the high school dropout rate. The regression is estimated for the 48 states that comprised the United States in 1938. The resulting regression is

$$EPI = -2.02 + 4.09HSG \qquad [1.7]$$

where EPI is the educational performance index and HSG is the high school graduation rate in 1938. The positive coefficient on HSG implies that, on average, states with high (low) high school graduation rates in 1938 had a high (low) educational performance index in the 1990s. In other words, performance in the 1990s is positively related to high school graduation rates in 1938, consistent with the idea that relative performance of states did not change greatly over time.

Example 1.2—Women in Films and Box Office Receipts

It has been noted that female actresses are underrepresented in films. To explore a possible explanation as to why this might be the case, Lindner, Lindquist, and Arnold (2015) examine whether the presence of at least two women playing important roles in a film results in lower box office receipts. If this is the case, the result would suggest that the underrepresentation, at least in part, is due to lower public interest in such films. The authors estimate a regression in which the dependent variable is box office receipts and the explanatory variable is a measure of the presence of women in the film. They use data for 964 films for the period 2000–2009, and obtain the following regression equation:

$$R = 84.843 - 11.356F \qquad [1.8]$$

where R is the box office receipts (in millions of dollars) of a film and F is a measure of the gender representation in the movie. The negative coefficient of -11.356 implies that the presence of important roles by females in movies is associated with lower box office receipts, consistent with the premise that the public is less interested in seeing movies that feature females.

Example 1.3—Using Measures of Extremities to Determine Height

Forensic scientists can face the challenging task of determining the identity of individuals from commingled human remains. One variable that can be of use in determining identity is the approximate height of the presumed deceased. Linear regression analysis is one method that has been used to infer the height of the deceased when only measures of extremities, such as hands or feet, are available. For example, Krishan, Kanchan, and Sharma (2012) obtained the following result when the height (HT) of 123 females living in Himachal Pradesh State in India was regressed on the length of their feet (FT), where each variable was measured in centimeters:

$$HT = 74.820 + 3.579FT \qquad [1.9]$$

The results imply that each additional centimeter of foot length is associated with 3.579 cm. of additional height.

The Linear Correlation Coefficient

In the first part of this chapter, we demonstrated how regression analysis can be used to summarize the relationship between a dependent and an independent variable. We turn now to an explanation of descriptive statistics designed to evaluate (1) the degree of association between variables and (2) how well the independent variable has explained the dependent variable. The *correlation coefficient* measures the degree of linear association between two variables.[13] To understand what statisticians mean by linear association, consider Figure 1.4, which has the same 50 points as Figure 1.1. The average (or mean) level of food consumption is represented by the horizontal dashed line, while the vertical solid line represents the mean level of income. The two lines divide the figure into the four quadrants denoted by Roman numerals. Levels of C that are greater than the average of \$8,795.14 lie above the dashed line in quadrants I and II, while less than average levels lie below, in quadrants III and IV. Similarly, income levels greater than the

---

[13]There are several different measures of correlation, depending on the nature of the variables. An explanation of the necessary conditions for calculating the correlation coefficient discussed here is beyond the scope of the book.

average lie to the right of $72,321.72 in quadrants I and IV, while those less than average lie to the left in quadrants II and III.

Figure 1.4 demonstrates that a majority of the points in the sample lie in quadrants I and III. Because of this pattern, the variables C and I are said to be *positively correlated*. Put differently, C and I are said to be positively correlated when C's above (below) the mean value of food consumption, denoted $\bar{C}$, are associated with I's above (below) the mean value of income, denoted $\bar{I}$. On the other hand, if the C's below $\bar{C}$ had been associated with the I's above $\bar{I}$ (and vice versa), one would have said that the variables were *negatively correlated*. The reader should be able to demonstrate that in this case the data points would have been clustered in quadrants II and IV. Other possibilities exist: If the data points had been spread fairly evenly throughout the four quadrants or in just quadrants II and III or just III and IV, one would have said that C and I were *uncorrelated*.

The particular descriptive statistic that measures the degree of linear association between two variables is called the *correlation coefficient* and is denoted r.[14] Although we don't provide the proof, r always lies between

Majority of points in I + III = (+) association

Figure 1.4 Linear Correlation Analysis: The Food Expenditure Problem

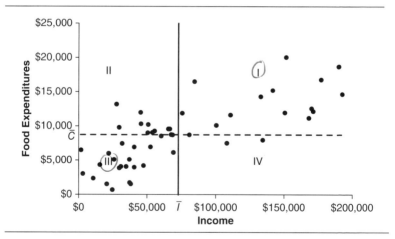

[14]The formula for the correlation coefficient is $\sum[(x_i - \bar{x})(y_i - \bar{y})] / \sqrt{\sum(x_i - \bar{x})^2 \sum(y_i - \bar{y})^2}$, where $\bar{x}$ and $\bar{y}$ are the means of x and y, respectively. An alternative, but equivalent formula is $[n\sum x_i y_i - (\sum x_i)(\sum y_i)] / [\sqrt{n\sum x_i^2 - (\sum x_i)^2} \sqrt{n\sum y_i^2 - (\sum y_i)^2}]$. The former is more intuitive, while the latter is used in most statistics books.

the values of −1 and +1 (−1.0 ≤ r ≤ +1.0). When there is little linear association between two variables (when two variables are relatively unrelated), r is close to zero. In the presence of strong correlation, r is close to 1 (+1 for positive correlation, −1 for negative correlation).

Although the correlation coefficient is 0.756 (a positive number) for the food example, where it was hypothesized that changes in income caused changes in food expenditures, the presence of either positive or negative correlation does not necessarily indicate causality. In particular, because the correlation coefficient measures only the degree of association between two variables, it might reflect a cause-and-effect relationship; however there are other reasons besides causality that can influence the size of the coefficient. Variables may also appear correlated if both variables affect each other, if the two variables are both related to a third variable, or if the variables are systematically associated by coincidence.

An example of the first reason that both variables might affect each other is that IQ scores and student achievement scores are likely to be positively correlated. Although it seems reasonable that IQ influences achievement, many educators believe that this is only part of the story. Indeed, it seems likely that the IQ measure also reflects the level of achievement. An example of the second reason, that is, that the variables are related to a third variable, is the positive correlation that exists across cities between the number of churches and the number of bars. Although churches may spring up in response to bars (or bars in response to churches), the positive association most likely results because both variables are related to some other variable, such as population. A good example of the last reason, that the variables are related by coincidence, is the positive correlation of 0.943 found between the number of letters in the names of the teams in the Central Division of the National Baseball League and the number of wins during the 2014 regular season.[15]

The Coefficient of Determination

Recall that for any problem, the regression line is defined to be the line lying closest to the data points (closest in the sense that the line minimizes the sum of the squared errors term). Often, for comparative purposes, it is useful to know just how close is "close"; in other words, it is helpful to be able to evaluate what is referred to as the *goodness of fit* of the regression line.

---

[15]The correlation coefficient in this case is, of course, affected greatly by the fact that the Cardinals had a good year while the Cubs and Reds did not. For the Western Division, the equivalent correlation coefficient is −0.592.

18

An intuitive feeling for what is meant by goodness of fit is given in Figure 1.5, in which two distinct sets of data points have been plotted along with the two lines that minimize the sum of the squared errors. The two regression lines have the same values for a and b. The data points in panel A of Figure 1.5 are clearly closer to the regression line than the data points in panel B.

Figure 1.5   Comparison of Goodness of Fit for Two Regression Lines

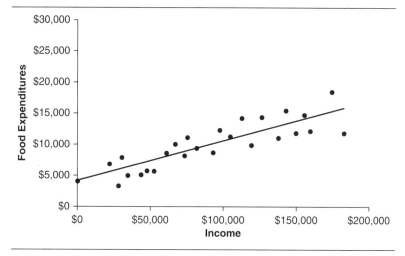

Panel A: Regression Equation With High R^2

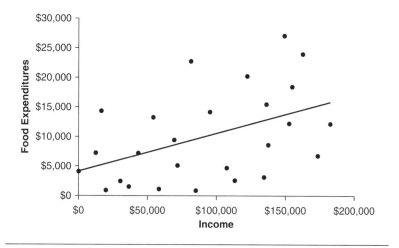

Panel B: Regression Equation With Low R^2

The measure of relative closeness used by statisticians for evaluating goodness of fit is called the *coefficient of determination*. Because of its relationship to the correlation coefficient, this measure is generally referred to as the R^2. (The coefficient of determination is actually the square of the correlation coefficient, and is commonly referred to as "R squared.") The R^2 statistic measures closeness as the percentage of total variation in the dependent variable explained by the regression line. Formally, the measure is defined as

$$R^2 = \sum_{i=1}^{n}(\hat{C}_i - \overline{C})^2 / \sum_{i=1}^{n}(C_i - \overline{C})^2 \qquad [1.10]$$

To measure variation in a family's food consumption, we want some common base from which to measure differences in C. To the extent that families consume more or less than the mean food consumption, denoted $\overline{C}$, there is variation in food consumption. Thus we use $\overline{C}$ as the base for measuring variations in C between families.

The denominator of equation 1.10 is a measure of the total variation in the dependent variable about its mean value $\overline{C}$. For example, consider a household with an income of $21,400 and observed consumption of $6,100 (the 15th observation shown in Table 1.1). Since the mean value of consumption is $8,795.14, the observed variation of C from the mean is −$2,695.14 for this observation (−$2,695.14 = 6,100 − 8,795.14). So that negative variations do not cancel positive variations, the individual variations are squared before they are summed.

The numerator of equation 1.10 is a measure of the total variation explained by the regression line. For example, from regression equation 1.6, it follows that the best estimate of food consumption for the family with an income of $21,400 is $5,524.81 ($5,524.81 = 4,155.21 + 0.064($21,400). Since this is −$3,270.33 from the mean (−$3,270.33 = $5,524.81 − $8,795.14), it is said that −$3,270.33 is the variation explained by the regression line for this observation. The total explained variation is found by summing the squares of these variations for the entire sample.

For the food expenditure problem, the value of the R^2 is 0.571, and one can say that the regression line explains 57.1% of the total variation in food expenditures. Stated somewhat differently, it can be said that 57.1% of the variation (about the mean) in the dependent variable has been explained by (or is attributable to) variation (about the mean) in the independent variable.

Notice that if the data points were all to lie directly on the regression line, the observed values of the dependent variable would be equal to the predicted values, and the R^2 would be equal to 1. As the independent variable explains less and less of the variation in the dependent variable, the value of R^2 falls toward zero. Hence, as would be expected, the R^2 for the data in panel A of Figure 1.5, 0.741, is greater than that for the data in panel B of Figure 1.5, 0.209.

Regression and Correlation

It is important to note that linear regression, the correlation coefficient, and the coefficient of determination are all related but that they provide different amounts of information and are based on different assumptions. First, as indicated previously, the coefficient of determination is simply the square of the correlation coefficient. An examination of Figure 1.4 should also convince the reader that if two variables are positively (negatively) correlated, the regression coefficient, that is, b, will have a positive (negative) sign.[16]

While this general relationship between r and b will always hold, one might ask if one of these two measures provides more information than the other. The answer is that the regression coefficient is more informative, since it indicates by how much and in what direction the dependent variable changes as the independent variable changes, whereas the correlation coefficient indicates only whether or not the two variables move in the same or opposite directions and the degree of linear association. This additional information from regression is obtained, however, at the cost of a more restrictive assumption—namely, that the dependent variable is a function of the independent variable. It is not necessary to designate which is the dependent and which the independent variable when a correlation coefficient is obtained.

Summary

Linear regression analysis provides a method for summarizing how one variable, referred to as the independent variable, explains variation in another, referred to as the dependent variable. In simple linear regression analysis, the relationship takes the form of a straight line defined by the slope coefficient and the intercept coefficient. The specific line chosen among all possible lines to summarize the relationship between the two variables is the one that minimizes the sum of the squared errors. The coefficient of determination provides a measure of the goodness of fit between the regression line and the data used to estimate the regression line. In the next chapter we examine how the same technique can be used to explore the relationship between a dependent variable and several independent variables.

---

[16]The relationship between the regression coefficient and the correlation coefficient can be shown to be $b = r(s_y / s_x)$, where s_y is the standard deviation of the dependent variable and s_x is the standard deviation of the independent variable. Standard deviation is a measure of the dispersion, about the mean, of the distribution of some variable. The further the values of a variable are spread out from the mean, the greater the value of the standard deviation. The formula for the standard deviation is $\sqrt{\sum (X_i - \bar{X})^2 / (n-1)}$, where n is the number of observations.

CHAPTER 2. MULTIPLE LINEAR REGRESSION

Introduction

In Chapter 1, variations in the dependent variable were attributed to changes in only a single independent variable. This is known as *simple* (or *bi-variate*) *linear regression.* Yet theories very frequently suggest that several factors simultaneously affect a dependent variable. *Multiple linear regression analysis* is a method for estimating the effects of several factors concurrently.

There are numerous occasions where the use of multiple regression analysis is appropriate. In economics it has been used to estimate how the demand for gasoline responds to changes in prices and income (Arzaghi and Squalli 2015). The likelihood that an unemployed individual will double up (share living arrangements) with family or friends depends on many factors, including the individual's education level and age (Wiemers 2014). The determinants of whether US senators vote in favor of a specific economic policy include both the views of their political constituency and the role of campaign funding (Hall and Shultz 2015). The likelihood that an unemployed individual will find employment depends on the person's age and education, as well as whether the person has volunteered at a nonprofit organization (Spera et al. 2015). The possible link between the commission of violent crimes and attendance at strongly violent movies is examined by Dahl and DellaVigne (2009) using multiple regression techniques.

This chapter shows that multiple linear regression is a straightforward extension of simple linear regression. The chapter also discusses an alternative measure of the effect of independent variables on a dependent variable, called the beta coefficient; it also introduces an alternative to the R^2, called the *adjusted* R^2.

Estimating Regression Coefficients

In the food consumption example, only a single variable, income, was hypothesized as a determinant of family food expenditures. One recognizes, however, that even though two families have identical incomes, their food expenditures may differ greatly. For example, the families may differ in size, in the availability of homegrown items that can decrease out-of-pocket food costs, or in taste. Therefore, it is reasonable to hypothesize that other variables, in addition to income, affect the amount spent on food. One likely hypothesis is that food expenditures are positively related to the family's size, denoted S. Multiple linear regression analysis can be used to estimate the effect of S on food consumption while at the same time taking into account the effect of income.

The concept of multiple regression analysis is identical to that of simple regression analysis, except that two or more independent variables are used simultaneously to explain variations in the dependent variable. When family size is added to income to explain food consumption, the newly hypothesized relation can be written as

$$C = \alpha + \beta_1 I + \beta_2 S \qquad [2.1]$$

where α, β_1, and β_2 must be estimated from observed values of consumption, income, and family size. For any observed combination of values for I and S, it is still desired to find values for the coefficients that minimize the distance between the corresponding observed and estimated values of C.

A graphical presentation of these concepts is now more difficult, since with two independent variables, three-dimensional drawings are required. Minimizing distance in this context means minimizing the length of line segments drawn between the observed values of the dependent variable and its estimated value lying on the plane corresponding to $C = \alpha + \beta_1 I + \beta_2 S$. Algebraically, this means finding the values of a, b_1, and b_2 that minimize the value of

$$\sum_{i=1}^{n}(C_i - a - b_1 I_i - b_2 S_i)^2 \qquad [2.2]$$

As in the case of simple regression analysis, a technique exists that ensures that the resulting estimates of α, β_1, and β_2 are those that minimize the sum of squared errors and thus give the best estimates of the coefficients. When this technique is applied to the data in Table 1.1, the estimated regression equation obtained is

$$C = 2962.95 + 0.055I + 825.78S \qquad [2.3]$$

Interpretation of these results is similar to simple regression analysis. For example, the coefficients derived from the data indicate that the estimate of food consumption for a family of four with an income of $30,000 is $7,916.07, since $7,916.07 = $2,962.95 + 0.055($30,000) + 825.78(4).[1]

More generally, the estimated coefficient on any independent variable estimates the effect of that variable *while holding the other independent variable(s)*

---

[1]The constant term, 2,962.95 suggests that families with zero income and size zero would still purchase $2,962.95 of food. Obviously, families of zero size do not exist; hence direct interpretation of the constant term in this case is nonsensical. In fact, there are many instances in regression analysis where the constant term has no real-world meaning. Nevertheless, estimation of a constant is necessary to ensure that the squared error term is minimized. The lack of direct interpretability of estimated coefficients of the constant term explains why authors sometimes do not report them in their results, as is the case in Example 2.2 below.

constant. This allows one to isolate the effect of just one variable on the dependent variable, holding the other variable(s) constant. For example, the coefficient on income in a multiple linear regression equation that estimates how the demand for gasoline responds to changes in price and income shows how gas consumption changes when income changes but price does not.

The results shown in equation 2.3 indicate that holding income constant, an increase of one in family size is associated with an $825.78 increase in food consumption.[2] Similarly, the results suggest that a dollar increase in income will increase food expenditures by 5.5 cents, holding family size constant. One can also consider the effect of a simultaneous change in S and I. For example, the estimated effect of a decrease in income of $1000 at the same time family size increases by one would be +$770.78 = 0.055(-1000) + 825.78(1). Notice too that the assumption of a linear regression equation means that a one-unit change in an independent variable has the same effect on the dependent variable at all values of the independent variable. For example, it is assumed that increasing family size from two to three has the same effect on food spending as if family size changes from, say, six to seven.

The coefficient on income in equation 2.3 is somewhat different from that reported in the simple linear regression case, where a one-dollar change in income resulted in a 6.4-cent change in food consumption. In some cases when another independent variable is introduced, this change in the value of the estimated coefficient may be large. This issue is discussed in more detail in Chapter 5.

Multiple regression results come closer to showing the pure effect of income on food consumption, since they explicitly recognize the influence of family size on food expenditures. It is for this reason that in formal studies it is not proper to exclude a variable such as family size when the theory indicates that the variable should be included. To simplify the presentation in Chapter 1, we did not follow the proper practice.

Finally, note that multiple linear regression is not limited to only two independent variables. Rather, it applies to any case when two or more independent variables are used simultaneously to explain variations in a single dependent variable.

Standardized Coefficients

In the multiple regression example, we noted by how much food consumption would increase for a given increase in income holding family size constant, and by how much food consumption would increase for a given increase in

---

[2]The reader can verify this proposition in the following way: The estimated value of C for a family of four with a $30,000 income is $7,916.07; for a family of five with a $30,000 income, C is estimated to be $8,741.85. This is a change in C of $825.78 = $8,741.85 − $7,916.07 associated with a one-unit change in S while holding income constant.

family size, holding income constant. A question that may arise is whether income or family size has the greater impact on food consumption. If we simply compared the size of the estimated parameters, it is obvious that b_2 is much greater than b_1, suggesting that family size has a greater effect on C or is more important than income. But that is not an appropriate comparison, since income is measured in dollars and family size is measured in persons. Comparing b_1 with b_2 is comparing the effect of a one-dollar increase in income to the effect of a one-person increase in family size. Relative to the range of income levels, a one-dollar change in income is very small, while for family size a one-person change is quite large.

Instead of determining the effect of a one-dollar increase in income or a one-person increase in family size, suppose we use a standardized unit to measure changes in income and family size. One such measure, the *standard deviation*, measures the dispersion of the values of a particular variable about its mean.[3] Look at the values of income and family size in Table 1.1, and notice that income is spread out over a wider range of values (from $1,200 to $192,220) than is family size (from 1 to 6). This dispersion is reflected in the standard deviations, which for income is $54,169.54 and for family size is 1.36. Thus, using the standard deviation as the unit of measure takes into account that a one-person change in family size is very important relative to the spread of values for family size, while a one-dollar change in income is rather unimportant relative to the dispersion in income levels.

Frequently researchers report *standardized coefficients*, also referred to as *beta coefficients* (do not confuse the beta coefficient with β, the population parameter). These standardized coefficients estimate the change in the dependent variable (measured in standard deviations, which in the case of the food example is $4,598.52) that results from a change of one standard deviation in the independent variables.

For the regression reported in equation 2.3, the standardized coefficients are 0.648 for income and 0.244 for family size.[4] Thus, increasing income by one standard deviation ($54,169.54), while holding family size constant, would increase food consumption by 0.648 standard deviations. Increasing family size by one standard deviation, holding income constant, would increase food consumption by 0.244 standard deviations. When viewed in this way, a change in income has a greater relative effect on food purchases

---

[3]See note 16 in Chapter 1 for the formula for the standard deviation.

[4]The formula for the standardized coefficient is given by $b_k \left(\dfrac{s_{x_k}}{s_y} \right)$, where b_k is the regression coefficient for variable k, s_{x_k} is the standard deviation of the kth independent variable, and s_y is the standard deviation of the dependent variable. For our regression, the standardized coefficient for income, 0.648, equals (0.055 * $54,169.54) / $4,598.52.

than does a change in family size, a finding opposite to that suggested by the regression coefficient.

Associated Statistics

Just as there is a great deal of similarity between the interpretation of simple and multiple regression coefficients, likewise there is similarity between many of the associated statistics for the two regression methods.

The *coefficient of multiple correlation*, often denoted as R, is similar to r, the coefficient of correlation, in that both measure the degree of associated variations in variables. Rather than measuring the association between two variables, the value of R indicates the degree to which variation in the dependent variable is associated with variations in the several independent variables taken simultaneously. Similarly, R^2, the *coefficient of determination*, measures the percentage of the variation in the dependent variable that is explained by variations in the independent variables taken together.

For regression equation 2.3, R^2 is 0.618, indicating that 61.8% of the variation in C about its mean is explained by variations in I and S about their respective means. Note that the addition of the second independent variable has increased the explanatory value of the regression over that of the simple linear regression case, which in Chapter 1 was shown to be 0.571. It is also evident, however, that even this regression equation does not explain all the variation in food expenditures.

It cannot be overemphasized that although the coefficient of determination is of interest, it should never be the sole determinant of the "goodness" or "badness" of a regression result. Selecting variables in order to maximize the R^2 is not the purpose of regression analysis. Although individuals use regression for other purposes, the purpose we stress in this book is exploration of hypothesized relationships between a dependent and independent variables. This means that the selection of independent variables should be based on the hypothesized relationship, not in order to enhance the goodness of fit.

The value of the coefficient of determination will never decrease (and almost always increases) when another variable is added to the regression. Although the additional variable may be of no use whatsoever in explaining variations in the dependent variable, it cannot reduce the explanatory value of the previously included variables. Thus, by carefully choosing additional independent variables, an investigator can increase the value of R^2 greatly without improving his or her knowledge of what affects the value of the dependent variable. For instance, the amount spent on food is partly reflective of the amount spent on meat. If a researcher were to include the dollar value of meat purchases as another independent variable, the R^2 statistic would probably increase greatly. However, such an equation would not increase our understanding of why food consumption expenditures differ across families. The moral is this: If a variable has no place in the theory, it should not be included in the regression analysis.

Since including additional variables can never decrease the value of R^2 and normally increases it, analysts commonly report the *adjusted R^2*, denoted $\bar{R}^2$. The formula is

$$\bar{R}^2 = \frac{(n-1)R^2 - k}{n - k - 1} \qquad [2.4]$$

where n is the number of observations and k is the number of independent variables in the regression equation.

This term is R^2 adjusted for the number of independent variables used in the regression (k). Thus it is possible that by adding another independent variable to the regression, the adjusted R^2 will decrease although R^2 actually increases. For this reason, $\bar{R}^2$ is sometimes used to determine whether including another independent variable increases the explanatory power of the regression more than would be expected purely due to chance.

Examples

We present two examples to illustrate how multiple regression analysis is used. Other examples are presented throughout the book. Bear in mind that the examples are not summaries of the articles cited, which commonly employ more extensive empirical analyses than are presented here.

Example 2.1—Contributions to Nonprofit
Organizations and the Mortgage Foreclosure Crisis

Voluntary contributions of money and/or time to nonprofit organizations are extremely common in the United States. Since these organizations commonly are intended to assist families in need, a question arises as to how the willingness and ability to contribute to such organizations respond to economic crises. On the one hand, there are likely to be greater needs for such support, which can prompt individuals to give more. On the other hand, economic crises can mean that persons who normally give to nonprofits will cut back on their giving in response to the crisis.

Rotolo, Wilson, and Dietz (2015) address this question using multiple regression analysis focusing on the proportion of the population in 120 metropolitan areas in the United States who say they have volunteered during each year from 2007 through 2009. The year 2008 saw a dramatic downturn in economic conditions throughout the country, with home mortgage foreclosures a centerpiece of the downturn. As a result, the principal independent variable of interest was the area's mortgage foreclosure rate during the year. The authors use several additional variables in their analysis under the expectation that these factors will also affect volunteerism. Since data include the years 2007–2009, an indicator is set equal to one for all 2008 data and another set equal to one for 2009 data. (These so-called dummy variables are explained in Chapter 4; here we ignore the interpretation of these particular results.)

The results, replicated in Table 2.1, reveal that mortgage foreclosures were positively associated with willingness to volunteer. (Standard errors, also shown in Table 2.1, are discussed in the following chapter.)

Table 2.1 Regression Results Showing Effects on Percent Volunteering

Variable	Regression Coefficient	Standard Error
Constant	−2.542	1.138
Foreclosure rate	1.474	0.413
Percentage of adults with BA or higher	0.804	0.326
Log median household income	0.192	0.104
Proportion of population black	3.215	0.849
Proportion of population Hispanic	−0.334	0.089
Unemployment rate	−0.167	0.096
Number of nonprofits per 1,000 population	0.039	0.025
Year 2008	−0.014	0.007
Year 2009	−0.002	0.007

Source: Adapted from Rotolo, Wilson, and Dietz (2015)

Example 2.2—Gender-Based Discrimination and Maternity Leave Policies

Countries around the world have vastly different policies regarding the number of days mandated for employers to provide maternity leave. Givati and Troiano (2012) use multiple linear regression to explain these cross-country differences. Their dependent variable is the number of mandated days of maternity leave in 2010, which, in their sample of 73 countries, ranges from 60 to 480. The authors are particularly interested in the possible effect that attitudes toward women in the labor force have on the legal mandates. To capture this attitudinal variable, they use an indicator from the World Values Survey, which asked survey respondents whether they agreed

Table 2.2   Regression Results Showing Effects on Days of Mandated
Maternity Leave Across Countries

Variable*	Regression Coefficient	Standard Error	Regression Coefficient	Standard Error
Men have more right to a job	−1.39	0.46	−0.80	0.37
GDP per capita			0.0001	0.0008
Government share of GDP			3.69	1.51
Population			−0.00005	0.00001
Share of women in parliament			1.59	1.17
Fertility			−30.51	9.48
R^2	0.14		0.25	

Source: Adapted from Givati and Troiano (2012)

*Although the authors estimated the intercept coefficients, they do not report them.

with the following statement: "When jobs are scarce, men should have more right to a job than women." The percentage of respondents within each country saying they agreed with this statement is used as their principal independent variable. However, other variables that might also affect the length of maternity leaves are also used in the analysis, including gross domestic product (GDP) per capita, government share of GDP, population, share of women in parliament, and the nation's fertility rate in 2010.

The results for their simplest model using only the attitudinal variable, along with the results from their most complex model, are shown in Table 2.2. The simple linear regression coefficient, −1.39, indicates that each additional percentage of the population that agrees with the statement that men have greater rights to jobs than women is associated with 1.39 fewer days of maternity leave. This single variable explains about 14% of the variation in maternity leaves across countries. The same negative relationship is shown in the more complex model. However, once other variables are included, the effect of the attitude variable is reduced in absolute size from −1.39 to −0.8 days. The regression also suggests that more populous countries and those with higher fertility rates mandate fewer days of maternity leave. Those with a higher percentage of women in parliament and a larger government share of GDP mandate more days. (Standard errors, also shown in Table 2.2, are discussed in the following chapter.)

Summary

Multiple regression analysis provides a method for summarizing the relationship between the dependent variable and two or more independent variables. The concept of multiple regression analysis is identical to that of simple regression analysis, except that two or more independent variables are used simultaneously to explain variations in the dependent variable. In this and the previous chapter, regression analysis has been approached as a way to describe the linear relationship between the dependent variable and the independent variables based on a sample of observations. Most researchers are, however, particularly interested in the question of whether the results can be generalized more broadly. To accomplish that objective, hypotheses must be tested statistically. We now turn to that topic.

CHAPTER 3. HYPOTHESIS TESTING

Introduction

In the food expenditure example, the hypothesis was advanced that family food consumption increases as income increases. Since the estimated coefficient was found to be a positive number, one might want to immediately conclude that we have proven our case. Unfortunately, drawing such inferences is not so easy, since our hypothesis concerns the *population* of all families, not just the 50 families in our *sample*. By way of example, although the coefficient on income is greater than zero for our food example, how confident are you that β, the population coefficient, is really greater than zero? Or, how confident would you be if, rather than basing the estimate on 50 households, the coefficient had been based on just 5 observations with incomes ranging from $5,000 to $10,000, or, if the estimated coefficient was 0.0001 and not 0.064? Hypothesis testing addresses these types of questions.

The hypothesis-testing procedure allows us to make statements about the entire population from our sample, not just statements about the particular sample we happen to draw. In order to make such inferential statements—that is, to infer from a random sample something about the population—we must develop some statistical theory. Therefore, before turning to testing hypotheses about population regression coefficients, we consider a slightly less complex example.

Suppose you were browsing the Internet and came across a document indicating that the average height of *all* students who attended your university or college in 1920 was 5 feet 4 inches (64 inches). Suppose further that you became interested in learning whether students enrolled in your school today are taller than students were in 1920. One way to attack this problem would be to measure the height of all students currently enrolled. While that procedure might work in a small liberal arts college with only a few hundred students, the task would be enormous if you were a student at a large state university. Fortunately, statistical theory allows one to make inferences about the mean height of the entire population of students using only information on the average height of students computed from a single random sample of the student population. After this inference has been made, comparisons can be made with the height for the population of students in 1920.

To continue with the example, suppose you measure the height of a *random sample* of 200 students and find that their mean height is 67 inches. Your sample of 200 is only one of many such samples that could be drawn from students on a large university campus. Therefore, even though the mean of 67 inches is greater than 64, you should not immediately conclude that today's student body is taller than the 1920 group. Instead, the hypothesis-testing procedure must account for the fact that, since your particular sample is only one of a large number of possible samples, the 67-inch mean is only one of a number of possible sample means. Some samples may yield sample means less than 64 inches.

The theory of hypothesis testing provides a method for making inferences about the entire population from sample data. The method recognizes that, since the inferential statement is based on sample information, we can never be totally certain of the validity of the inference about the population. Instead, we must allow for some probability that an incorrect conclusion has been drawn. Statistical theory allows us to define the likelihood of making such an incorrect inference. For example, based on the sample mean of 67 inches, you might conclude that today's student body is taller than the 1920 student body, but there is some chance, that is, some probability, that you have drawn an incorrect conclusion. Inferential statements based on sample data never yield conclusions about the population values that are 100% certain.

This chapter explains how hypotheses concerning regression coefficients can be tested and what the outcomes of those tests do and do not imply. We begin by providing a conceptual explanation for hypothesis testing, and we follow this with discussion of the hypothesis testing procedure. The chapter discusses as well the construction of what are called *confidence intervals* around estimated regression coefficients and the meaning of those intervals.

Concepts Underlying Hypothesis Testing

The basic approach of hypothesis testing is to *assume* that the anticipated or hypothesized outcome is not true. That is, in the case of the height of university students, you first assume that the average height of students today is still 64 inches. Then the hypothesis testing procedure, which relies on concepts from statistics, determines whether the sample evidence, that is, your sample mean of 67 inches, is sufficiently greater than 64 inches to allow you to conclude with a specified degree of confidence that the assumption is incorrect and that, yes, today's students are taller than students were in 1920.

This same idea carries over to our food consumption example. We suspect that there is a positive relationship between family income and the amounts that families annually spend on food, but for purposes of hypothesis testing, we initially *assume* that there is not a positive relationship between family income and food consumption. This essentially is assuming that the true population value of β is zero.[1] Next we compare the sample estimate

---

[1] Technically, we are assuming that β is ≤ 0.

of β with the assumed value, zero. If the difference between the two is sufficiently large, we will conclude that there is a positive relationship between income and food consumption.

The actual statistical procedure is more complicated than simply comparing the sample estimate with the assumed population value. To explain that procedure, we need some additional terminology from statistics along with an explanation of the underlying statistical theory. First, some terminology is in order. Statisticians call the assumed value of the population parameter the *null hypothesis*. The null hypothesis in the student height example is that the mean height of the population of students today is 64 inches. In the simple linear regression case, the null hypothesis is that the population value of β is zero.

The opposite of the null hypothesis is the *alternate*, or *research, hypothesis*. There are only two possible outcomes from the statistical test—either the null hypothesis cannot be rejected, or it is rejected in favor of the alternate. The testing procedure compares the sample estimate of the parameter with the assumed value of that parameter (the null hypothesis) and, if there is a sufficient difference between the two, the assumed null is *rejected* in favor of the alternate.

It is important to emphasize that whenever hypotheses are tested using sample data, the researcher can *never* be absolutely certain that the conclusion to reject the null hypothesis or not is the correct conclusion. Instead, the researcher must acknowledge that there is some probability, preferably a low one, that the conclusion is incorrect.

Statisticians call the probabilities of drawing incorrect conclusions from hypothesis testing the probabilities of Type I or Type II errors. The probability of a *Type I error* is defined to be the probability of *incorrectly rejecting the null hypothesis when the null is, in fact, true*. In the family income–food consumption case, a Type I error would occur if it is concluded, based on sample statistics, that there is a positive relationship between the two variables when, in fact, food expenditures for the population are not positively related to income. (Type I errors are sometimes referred to as "false positives.") The probability of a *Type II error* is defined to be the probability of *not rejecting the null hypothesis when, in fact, the null hypothesis is not correct*. (This is sometimes referred to as a "false negative.") Again, in the food example, suppose that the sample estimate of β is not sufficiently greater than zero for the researcher to conclude that the null hypothesis should be rejected. If, in fact, there *is* a positive relationship between the two variables in the population and the null hypothesis of no positive relationship is not true, the researcher would have committed a Type II error by failing to reject the null. (This is a complicated paragraph with several double negatives. It is worth spending a few minutes making sure you understand it.)

Of course, in the "real world" where the researcher does not know the value of the population parameter, there is no way of knowing whether a Type I or Type II error has occurred (although if the null is rejected, a Type I error *might* have been made, and if the null is not rejected, a Type II error *might* have been made). One approach many researchers take is to preset an acceptable level for the probability of a Type I error (rejecting the null hypothesis when it is, in fact, correct). A term commonly used for the probability of a Type I error is the *level of statistical significance,* sometimes referred to simply as *level of significance.*

You will, therefore, find many researchers reporting that their results show that the coefficient is "statistically significant" at, for example, the 0.05 level. By this they mean that there is at most a 5% (0.05) probability that they are wrong in rejecting the null hypothesis in favor of the alternate hypothesis. They acknowledge that there is a 5% chance that they have committed a Type I error. Or researchers may report that their results are "statistically significant" at the 0.01 level, meaning that there is only a 1% chance that they incorrectly rejected the null hypothesis and have a false positive. It is, however, incorrect for the researcher to state that the research hypothesis has been "proven" to be true. This is because the possibility always exists that an incorrect conclusion has been drawn regarding the population parameter from the sample evidence.

Two points need to be addressed at this stage. First, lowering the probability of making a Type I error increases the probability of making a Type II error (not rejecting the null hypothesis when it is actually false). Second, statistical significance does *not* necessarily mean that the results are economically, socially, politically, or practically "significant." That conclusion needs to be drawn by the researcher and the users of the research.

You may be concerned with what is an appropriate level of significance to look for in research papers. Unfortunately, there is no definitive answer to that question. In deciding how certain you want to be in rejecting the null hypothesis of no effect, it is important to consider the costs associated with making a Type I error. Consider, for example, the case where the Food and Drug Administration (FDA) rejects the null hypothesis that an experimental drug has no effect on a disease in favor of the alternate hypothesis that the drug does have an effect. Suppose that on this basis, the FDA permits the drug manufacturer to sell the drug, and the company does so. If a Type I error occurs (i.e., the FDA concludes that the drug is effective when it is not), the costs of the incorrect conclusion can be high both in terms of the costs patients pay for a treatment that does not work, as well as forgoing the use of another drug that may actually be effective. Of course, committing a Type II error would keep an effective drug off the market. Box 3.1, which shows the analogy between hypothesis testing and the criminal justice system, illustrates that society tries to minimize Type I errors in the criminal courts.

Box 3.1   Hypothesis Testing and the Justice System

Readers interested in the law may recognize a similarity between hypothesis testing and (at least in theory) the foundation of the criminal law system in the United States. It is commonly stated that a criminal is assumed to be not guilty unless there is strong evidence provided to the contrary. The assumption of not guilty is effectively the null hypothesis, with the alternate hypothesis being guilty. But in the court system there is always the possibility that an innocent defendant is (incorrectly) found to be guilty. To minimize the likelihood of punishing an innocent defendant, the justice system states that the evidence (based on observed data similar to sample statistics) must be sufficiently strong (i.e., in criminal cases it is "beyond a reasonable doubt") to lead to the finding of guilty. This is equivalent to minimizing the probability of a Type I error. But it's also recognized that if the system requires an extremely strong set of evidence leading to the finding of guilt, it will increase the likelihood that a person who actually did commit the crime for which he is being tried will be set free, that is, found not guilty. Again, this is equivalent to allowing for a Type II error. Note, too, that even the justice system does not state that a person found not guilty is, in fact, innocent of the crime. It is simply that the evidence was not sufficiently strong to render a finding of guilty.

We now turn to the statistical theory that underlies the hypothesis-testing procedure.

In the case of testing a hypothesis concerning a regression coefficient, the following test statistic, termed the *t ratio*, is computed:

$$t_r = (b - \beta_0)/s_b \qquad [3.1]$$

where b is the estimated value of the regression coefficient, β_0 is the null hypothesized value of the regression coefficient for the population, and s_b is the *standard error of the regression coefficient*.[2] (Note that some authors use the term *t statistic* rather than *t ratio*.) As suggested above, it is most common in linear regression studies for the null hypothesis to

---

[2]The discussion here focuses on a single regression coefficient such as would be obtained in a simple linear regression. In the case of multiple regression analysis, a separate t ratio is computed for each of the regression coefficients. Similarly, the same procedures can be used to test hypotheses about the intercept coefficient α.

be that the independent variable has no effect on the dependent variable, since researchers are generally interested in testing whether they can reject the null hypothesis of no effect in favor of the alternate hypothesis that the dependent variable *does* depend on the independent variable. In this case the null is $\beta_0 = 0$. Thus, in this case the t ratio is simply

$$t_r = b/s_b \qquad [3.2]$$

The questions that we need to address then are the following: (1) What is the s_b, (2) how is it determined, and (3) how do you use the t-ratio variable, t_r, to test hypotheses? We consider each of these questions in turn.

The Standard Error of the Regression Coefficient

Just as one could have multiple samples of student heights, it is possible to draw multiple samples of families from the same population. If we did this, the regression procedure outlined in Chapter 1 could be used to generate additional estimates of β, which, in all likelihood, would not be identical to our earlier estimate since the samples are different. Some of the b's, that is, the estimated values of β, will be very good in the sense that they lie close to the true, but unobservable, β. Others will be very bad in the sense that they lie some distance from β. The problem is that we have no way of knowing with certainty whether our b is a good or bad estimate of β.

The *standard error* of the estimated regression coefficient is a measure of the amount of variability that would be present among different b's estimated from independent samples drawn randomly from the same population. In essence, the standard error measures how sensitive the estimate of the parameter is to changes in a few observations in the sample. To understand what is meant by sensitive, consider Figure 3.1. Panel A presents two samples from population A, panel B presents two samples from population B, and panel C presents two samples from population C. In each case the ordinary least squares regression lines are also presented. The figure is constructed so that, with the exception of the observations identified with a diamond, the data points are the same for any given panel. That is, the data points in diagram A-2 are identical to those in A-1 except for the observations shown with a diamond; furthermore, the X values in both A-1 and A-2 are identical; only the corresponding Y values differ. The data points in diagrams B-1 and B-2 as well as C-1 and C-2 are similarly constructed. It is apparent that regression coefficients estimated from either population A or B are extremely sample-dependent. In both

Figure 3.1 Sensitivity of Regression Line to Changes in Observations

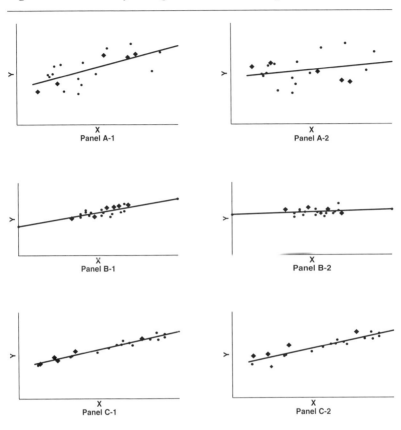

situations a change in a few of the observations results in a large change in the slope of the regression line and hence a large change in *b*. The data drawn from population C, however, are neither scattered nor clustered. In this instance, a change in a few of the observations will not alter *b* substantially.

What characteristics do the data in panels A and B have that do not occur in panel C? In panel A the amount of variability of the dependent variable *Y* (measured on the vertical axis) that cannot be attributable to variations in *X* is large relative to that shown in the data in panel C. In panel B the dispersion of the independent variable *X* is considerably less than the comparable range in the independent variable shown in panel C. Each of these characteristics is positively related to the standard error of a regression coefficient. These characteristics are reflected in the formula used to compute the standard error, s_b, in the case of simple linear regression.[3]

$$s_b = \frac{\sqrt{\frac{1}{n-2}\Sigma(Y_i - \hat{Y}_i)^2}}{\sqrt{\Sigma(X_i - \bar{X})^2}} , \qquad [3.3]$$

where $\hat{Y}_i$ is the value of Y for the ith observation that would be estimated by the regression line and $\bar{X}$ is the mean of X. A larger numerator (as illustrated in panel A of Figure 3.1) leads to a larger s_b. Likewise, a smaller denominator (as illustrated in panel B of Figure 3.1) results in a larger s_b.

Large standard errors mean that there is greater uncertainty about the value of the true population parameter β. Since the t ratio (see equations 3.1 and 3.2) includes the standard error in the denominator, a larger standard error will result in a smaller t ratio, which, as we will see, makes it less likely that the researcher can or should reject the null hypothesis. In Tables 2.1 and 2.2 (see Chapter 2), the columns labeled standard error provide the values of s_b for the estimated coefficients.

Because the standard error formula includes n, the number of observations used in the analysis affects the size of the standard error. Larger values of n will, all other things being the same, lead to smaller values for s_b. Intuitively this makes sense, since the estimate is based on more observations from the population. This, in turn, leads to a higher t ratio. It is, therefore, quite common for analyses based on large data sets containing several thousand observations to yield large t ratios, which make it more likely to reject the null hypothesis.

Some authors report t ratios, whereas others show the values of the standard error along with the estimated regression coefficients. These two values are all that are necessary to generate a t ratio as shown in equation 3.2.

The question then is how to use this t ratio to test hypotheses. Fortunately, statisticians have proven that the t ratio is distributed according to the probability distribution known as the Student's t distribution. We therefore need to understand the role of probability in the testing procedure and what the Student's t distribution looks like in order to proceed to the details of how hypotheses can be tested.

---

[3]The standard error formula in the case of multiple regression is more complex and not presented here. It depends on the variation of the dependent and independent variables in addition to correlations among the independent variables.

The Student's t Distribution

To recall the role that probability plays in the testing procedure, reconsider what has been said thus far about regression parameters. First, it has been stressed that the population parameter is not observed. Second, it has been noted that the estimate of the parameter from any sample is but one possible estimate; additional random samples from the population yield additional, probably different, estimates. Third, not all estimates are equally "close" to the population parameter. Finally, it is desired to draw inferences about the population parameter from one estimate of the parameter.

Box 3.2 Probability Distribution of a Discrete Random Variable

You may be aware of what is meant by a discrete probability density distribution. For example, you can create the probability distribution for the outcomes associated with tossing four "fair" coins that can result either in a "head" or in a "tail" on each toss where the probability that one coin will show heads is ½ or 0.5, with the same probability for showing tails. If four coins are tossed with the outcome on one coin not affecting the outcome on the other, the following is the probability distribution of the number of heads that will result:

# Heads	Probability of H
H = 0	1/16
H = 1	4/16
H = 2	6/16
H = 3	4/16
H = 4	1/16

We can use this probability density function to calculate, for example, the probability that the number of heads we get ranges between 0 and 2: The probability would be the sum 1/16 + 4/16 + 6/16, or 11/16. Note that the column of probabilities sums to 1, since the probability of getting any number of heads between 0 and 4 on four tosses is 1.

In the food consumption problem, we want to use the b of 0.064 to make inferences about the population β. Thus, we would like to know if 0.064 is one of the estimates that is close to β. A question of this nature can never be answered, since the value of the population parameter is unobservable and hence unknown. A statement can, however, be made regarding the probability of obtaining an estimate with a given degree of closeness to the assumed null hypothesized value of β. Analogously, statements can be made concerning the degree of closeness associated with a given probability. The reason such statements can be made is that statisticians have determined that, under commonly made assumptions, the probability distribution of the fraction $(b - \beta_0)/s_b$ (equation 3.1) follows the *Student's t distribution*.

The Student's t distribution[4] is a probability distribution for a continuous random variable that, in principle, can vary from negative infinity to positive infinity, with a density function that is centered on zero on a number line. When plotted, the t distribution looks very similar to the standard normal probability distribution with which you may be familiar. Both are "bell shaped" and centered at zero. Unlike a discrete random variable (see Box 3.2), determining the probability for the outcome of a continuous random variable requires the use of the calculus to find the area under the probability density function (see Box 3.3). Fortunately, others have already done this so that it is possible to easily determine the probability that a random variable takes on some range of outcomes by using prepared tables of the distribution.

Although the t distribution and standard normal probability distribution look somewhat similar, the t distribution has a second characteristic that does not occur in the normal distribution. This is known as the *degrees of freedom*, denoted *df*. While a full discussion of degrees of freedom is beyond the scope of this book, suffice it to say that the t distribution looks almost exactly like the normal distribution when the degrees of freedom are large, but is "flatter" with thicker tails than the standard normal when the degrees of freedom are small. (See Figure 3.2, which shows the shape of a t distribution with 48 degrees of freedom.) In the case of linear regression, the number of degrees of freedom is the total number of observations used to compute the regression coefficients less the number of coefficients that were estimated. Thus, for simple linear regression where both the slope and intercept have been estimated, $df = n - 2$, where n is the number of observations used in the data set. For multiple regression $df = n -$ (number of independent variables used) $- 1$ (for the intercept).

To return to the question of testing hypotheses, recall that statisticians have proved that the t ratio, $t_r = (b - \beta_0)/s_b$, is distributed as the Student's t distribution (with *df* as shown above). Assuming that the null hypothesis is true, this means that we can determine the probability that we would

---

[4]Notice that this is not expressed as "Students" with the apostrophe after the s. Instead, it was developed by an Englishman, William Gosset, who published under the pseudonym, Student. Gosset's employer, Guinness Brewery, required that he use a pseudonym.

Figure 3.2   t Distribution With 48 Degrees of Freedom

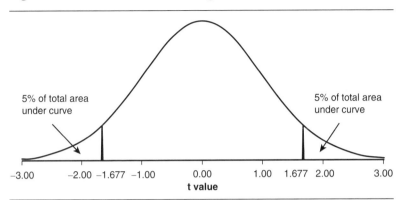

find a t ratio at least as large as the ratio obtained from the sample. That probability will be the area under the t distribution curve to the right of the t ratio. If the estimated coefficient, *b*, lies a long distance from the null hypothesized value of *β* (relative to the size of the standard error), the t ratio will be large. But this means that there is a small probability that such a large t ratio would be obtained *if the null hypothesis is correct*. In such an instance, the researcher can be reasonably confident in rejecting the null hypothesis in favor of the alternate.

Box 3.3   More Information About the t Distribution

While the underlying mathematics of the t distribution are more complex than developed here, a picture of what the t distribution looks like is useful. The distribution shown in Figure 3.2 is bell shaped and centered at zero. The construction of the distribution is such that the total area under the curve is equal to 1. Hence, any portion of the area under the curve can be thought of as some proportion of 1. The exact shape of the t distribution depends on the degrees of freedom, with fewer degrees of freedom resulting in a flatter bell-shaped curve (still centered at zero). For each possible *df*, statisticians have computed the proportion of the area under the curve lying on either side of any value of *t*.

The t distribution shown in Figure 3.2 represents the t distribution associated with 48 degrees of freedom. For a *t* equal to 1.677, 5% of

(Continued)

42

(Continued)

the area under the curve will lie to the right of 1.677, and 95% of the area will lie to the left of it. Since probabilities are always expressed as positive fractions in the range from zero to one, we can say that the probability is 0.05 that a variable, which in this case is b / s_b, distributed as a t distribution (with 48 degrees of freedom) will be greater than 1.677, and the probability is 0.95 that the variable will be less than 1.677.

Since the t distribution is symmetric around zero, it is also the case that 5% of the area under the curve will lie to the left of −1.677 (in the left hand tail, to the left of zero) and 95% of the area will be to the right of −1.677. Thus the total area to the right of +1.677 *plus* that to the left of −1.677 is 10% of the total area under the curve.

Figure 3.3, which is again a t distribution with 48 *df*, also illustrates an area that is 10% of the total area under the curve. However, since the area is concentrated in one tail, a *t* of only 1.299 leaves 10% of the area to its right.

There are web-based programs available on the Internet that generate critical values for a t distribution for any specified degrees of freedom and levels of significance. See, for example, the application: http://homepage.stat.uiowa.edu/~mbognar/applets/t.html

Figure 3.3   t Distribution With 48 Degrees of Freedom; 10% of Area in One Tail

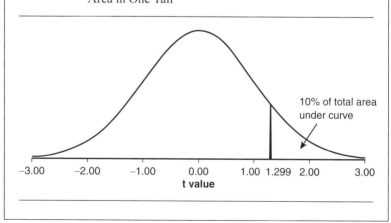

How large must the t ratio be in order to reject the null hypothesis? This depends on two variables—the degrees of freedom and the probability that one accepts for committing a Type I error. This probability is referred to as the *level of significance* at which the null hypothesis is being tested. Shown in Appendix B are the *critical values* of the t ratio that must be exceeded in order to reject the null hypothesis. Two things are notable from the entries there. First, for a given number of degrees of freedom, a researcher must obtain a higher value for the t ratio in order to conclude, with a lower probability of a Type I error, that the null hypothesis is to be rejected. But that should seem logical since, in order to decrease the probability of making a Type I error, the researcher must have stronger evidence to reject the assumed null hypothesis. Second, for a given level of significance, as the degrees of freedom increase, a smaller t ratio is required in order to reject the null hypothesis.

We illustrate this with the food consumption example where the null hypothesis is denoted H_0: $\beta \leq 0$ and the alternate is H_A: $\beta > 0$. Since the estimated coefficient on income is 0.064 in the simple linear regression reported on in Chapter 1, and the standard error is 0.008, the t ratio is 8.00. Appendix B shows that with $df = 48$ and a 5% probability of committing a Type I error, the critical value for the t distribution is 1.677. Since 8.00 > 1.677, we can comfortably reject the null hypothesis that the coefficient on income is equal to zero. Indeed, the large t ratio allows us to also reject the null hypothesis at the 0.005 level of significance, since the critical t value shown for 0.005 in Appendix B is 2.682 and the t ratio 8.00 is much larger than that.

You will often read statements that say that the estimated coefficient on some independent variable is "statistically significantly different from zero at the 5% level." What this means is that there is less than a 5% probability that a Type I error will be committed by rejecting the null hypothesis that β equals zero. Similar statements are made for lower or higher levels of significance.

Example 2.2 focused on factors that could affect the number of days of mandated maternity leave. It might be expected that the number of women serving in parliament would have a positive effect on that dependent variable. The regression coefficient on the variable is +1.59; however, the standard error of 1.17 produces a t ratio of 1.36. Since 1.36 is less than 1.668 (the value of the t from the table for 66 degrees of freedom and 5% level of significance), you would *not* reject at the 0.05 level of significance the null hypothesis that the number of women in parliament has no positive effect on the number of mandated days of maternity leave.

Left-Tail Tests

The preceding procedure is sometimes known as a "right-tail" test since the comparison of the t ratio with the Student's t distribution is in the right-hand "tail" of the t distribution where the critical values of t are greater than zero, that is, positive. The null hypothesis that $\beta \leq 0$ would be rejected only if the estimated coefficient is a sufficiently large positive number. However, sometimes researchers are interested in relationships where it is expected that the estimated coefficient will be a negative number. For example, in the food consumption case it was anticipated that consumers who tended their own garden would spend less on food than consumers not in that situation. In this instance an appropriate null hypothesis would be $\beta \geq 0$ with the alternate being $\beta < 0$.

Rejection of the null hypothesis will require a sufficiently large negative number. Again, a t ratio can be formed as in equation 3.2, $t_r = b/s_b$. If, as the researcher anticipates, the estimated coefficient is a negative number, then the t ratio is also negative, since the standard error is always positive.[5] The explanation of the t distribution above and in Box 3.3 noted that it is symmetric around zero. This means that for any value of t taken from the t distribution, call it t^*, the area under the t distribution to the right of a positive t^* will be the same as the area to the left of negative t^*. In this case the researcher can use the absolute value of t^* and rely on the same decision rule as indicated above, that is, if $|t_r| > t^*$ found in the table for the appropriate degrees of freedom and the level of significance chosen to test the hypothesis, the null can be rejected.

Two-Tail Tests

Occasionally theory does not suggest the direction of the relationship between the dependent and independent variables. In this case a *two-tail test* is appropriate.[6] Such might be the case in Example 1.2, where it is possible that female presence in a movie could either increase or decrease ticket sales, or in Example 2.1, where it is not clear whether the relationship between voluntary contributions to nonprofit organizations is positively or negatively related to the foreclosure rate.

---

[5]If the estimated coefficient is *positive,* the researcher can immediately conclude that the null hypothesis that $\beta \geq 0$ cannot be rejected. The null that $\beta \geq 0$ can be rejected only if the coefficient is a sufficiently "large" negative number.

[6]Although it is beyond the scope of this book, it can be shown that when there is strong theoretical or a prioi rationale for the sign on a coefficient to be positive (or negative), a one-tail test will lead to a lower likelihood of a Type II error for a particular level of significance.

In fact, it is quite common for researchers not to specify a particular direction for the alternate hypothesis and instead simply to test the null hypothesis $\beta = 0$ versus the alternate hypothesis that $\beta \neq 0$. In this case the null hypothesis is rejected if the estimated coefficient is either sufficiently larger than zero or sufficiently smaller than zero, that is, a sufficiently large negative number.

To carry out the test, the researcher again computes a t ratio, $t_r = b/s_b$. But since the null is rejected if the coefficient is either positive or negative, testing at a particular level of significance, for example, 0.05, requires that the rejection regions under the t distribution be equally divided between the two tails. Thus, there will be 0.025 area under the right hand tail of the distribution and similarly 0.025 area under the left-hand tail (for the degrees of freedom available in the particular problem). Note that this means that the probability associated with a specific t value for a one-tail test corresponds to one half the level of probability for the same specific t value for a two-tail test. Or, for a comparable probability, the t value for a two-tail test is larger than the t value for a one-tail test.

In Example 2.1 it was noted that the authors of the article were uncertain whether voluntary contributions to nonprofit organizations would increase or decrease as the economy declined. Thus, a two-tail test is appropriate for the null hypothesis that $\beta = 0$ and the alternate that $\beta \neq 0$. The estimated coefficient on the independent variable "foreclosure rate" was +1.474 with a standard error of 0.413. This yields a t ratio of 3.469 (=1.474/0.413). Since there were 360 observations, and 10 coefficients including the intercept were estimated, $df = 350$. With that many degrees of freedom, the entries in Appendix B show that the null hypothesis that the foreclosure rate has no effect (positive or negative) on voluntarism can be rejected at the 0.01 level of significance since the value of t for a two-tail test and $df = 350$ is 2.590, and 3.469 exceeds this.[7] In fact, although Appendix B does not show it, this null hypothesis could be rejected at the 0.001 level of significance.

Box 3.4 summarizes the steps in testing hypotheses regarding regression coefficients under the assumption that the regression coefficients have been estimated from a sample randomly drawn from a population. Box 3.5 discusses how the results of such tests are commonly reported in academic journals.

---

[7]You will note that the values of the t from the table with infinite df is 2.576 at 0.5%, which is very close to the t for $df = 350$. Thus, in large samples it is common to use the value of the t taken from the table with infinite df.

Box 3.4   Steps in Testing Hypotheses About a Single Regression Coefficient

Right-Tail Test

1. Specify hypotheses—Null $H_0: \beta \leq \beta_0$ Alternate $H_A: \beta > \beta_0$

2. Compute t ratio $t_r = (b - \beta_0)/s_b$, where b is the estimated coefficient and s_b is the standard error of that coefficient.

3. Determine degrees of freedom, $df = n -$ (number of independent variables) $- 1$, where n is the number of observations used in the analysis.

4. Find critical value of t from table of the t distribution with df degrees of freedom and level of significance at which you wish to test the null hypothesis.

5. If t ratio $> t$ from the table, reject the null hypothesis. If t ratio $< t$ from the table, do not reject the null.

Left-Tail Test

1. Specify hypotheses—Null $H_0: \beta \geq \beta_0$ Alternate $H_A: \beta < \beta_0$

2. Compute t ratio $t_r = (b - \beta_0)/s_b$, where b is the estimated coefficient and s_b is the standard error of that coefficient.

3. Determine degrees of freedom, $df = n -$ (number of independent variables) $- 1$, where n is the number of observations used in the analysis.

4. Find critical value of t from table of the t distribution with df degrees of freedom and level of significance at which you wish to test the null hypothesis.

5. If absolute value of t ratio $> t$ from the table, reject the null hypothesis. If absolute value of t ratio $< t$ from the table, do not reject the null.

Two-Tail Test

1. Specify hypotheses—Null $H_0: \beta = \beta_0$ Alternate $H_A: \beta \neq \beta_0$

2. Compute t ratio $t_r = (b - \beta_0)/s_b$, where b is the estimated coefficient and s_b is the standard error of that coefficient.

3. Determine degrees of freedom, $df = n -$ (number of independent variables) $- 1$, where n is the number of observations used in the analysis.

4. Find critical value of t from table of the t distribution with df degrees of freedom and one-half the level of significance at which you wish to test the null hypothesis.

5. If absolute value of t ratio $> t$ from the table, reject the null hypothesis. If absolute value of the t ratio $< t$ from the table, do not reject the null.

Confidence Intervals

Confidence intervals are very closely related to the statistical theory underlying hypothesis testing. A confidence interval is constructed around the estimated regression coefficient and has the property that it has a given probability that the resulting interval will include within its bounds the true population parameter, β. Specifically, the formula for a confidence interval is

$$b \pm (t)(s_b) \quad\quad\quad [3.4]$$

where s_b is the estimated standard error for the regression coefficient and t is a value chosen from a t distribution table. (Note that this t is not the t ratio as discussed above.) Again, the value of t from the table will depend on two variables—the degrees of freedom associated with the number of observations used, and the level of confidence that the researcher wishes to have about the probability that the resulting interval encompasses the true, but unknown, value of β. For example, if the researcher wishes to have an interval that has a 95% chance of including the true value of β, with 48 degrees of freedom, the critical value of t to be used in formula 3.4 is 2.011. In each instance the t value is such that 2.5% of the area under the t-distribution lies to the right (left) of +2.011 (−2.011).

An interval constructed in that manner has a 95% chance that it might contain the true value of β, but a 5% chance that it does not encompass β. Keep in mind that the true value of β does not change; the uncertainty is whether or not the constructed interval happens to capture it. In the food expenditure example in Chapter 1, the 95% confidence interval is 0.064 ± (2.011)(0.008) or (0.048, 0.080). Thus with 95% confidence we would say that, based on our simple linear regression estimate, an additional dollar of income could result in additional spending on food of between 4.8 cents and 8.0 cents.

If the researcher wishes to have a greater likelihood that the interval constructed includes the true population parameter, for example, a 99% level of confidence, the appropriate t (again with 48 degrees of freedom) is 2.682. Thus, in order to be more confident, the researcher will have to give up precision in the interval, since it will be substantially wider than the one with a 95% level of confidence. But, just as with the case of hypothesis testing discussed above, the researcher can never be absolutely certain that the confidence interval does indeed encompass the true β. It either does or it does not; the only thing that can be determined is the probability that it does.[8]

Confidence intervals can, therefore, also be used to test null hypotheses (most easily for two-tail tests). The test procedure is as follows: Reject the null hypothesized value of β with a specified level of significance in favor of the alternate if the null is not included in the confidence interval. On the other hand, if the null hypothesized value of β is included within the interval, do not reject the null hypothesis. By way of example, a 95% confidence interval is constructed in such a way that there is a 95% chance that it will contain the population parameter. If the confidence interval does not contain the null hypothesis, we can be reasonably confident in rejecting the null in favor of the alternate. We say that the variable is significant at the 5% level because the probability is only 5% that we have rejected the null in favor of the alternate when the null is indeed true.

Box 3.5   Reporting Results of Hypothesis Tests

Different researchers and academic journals report the results of hypothesis tests in different ways. Some authors will report the value of the t ratio or the standard error next to or below the coefficient. In some cases the level of significance is indicated by additional markings such as asterisks or other special characters placed next to the coefficients and defined in a footnote to the table. For example, an author might place an asterisk next to a coefficient and show in the table footnote that the coefficient is statistically significant at better than some level, such as 5%.

In some cases authors of journal articles or research papers do not report whether their null hypothesis is rejected at a specific level of

---

[8]You may be very familiar with confidence intervals based on media reports of opinion polls of voters prior to elections. They often report the percentage of respondents favoring a candidate but then add that, due to the uncertainty associated with sampling, readers should add and subtract, for example, three percentage points from the reported percentage. What is sometimes not added is that even then the resulting interval has only a specified chance of including the true proportion of voters favoring the candidate.

significance, for example, 0.05 or 0.01. Instead, the researcher reports the estimated probability of having committed a Type I error, that is, the level of significance. This is often reported as the "p-value" or "prob-value" or, sometimes, it is simply called the level of significance. For example, if a researcher reports a p-value of 0.035, it should be interpreted to mean that the null hypothesis *can* be rejected at the 0.04 level of significance but not be rejected at the 0.03 level. Another interpretation of the p-value is that it represents the probability of obtaining the reported regression coefficient even though the null hypothesis is true.

As is shown in Appendix C, statistical packages that compute linear regression coefficients provide the estimates of α and β along with the standard errors but also compute the corresponding values of a t ratio and a p-value. Users of such programs should be aware that the resulting p-value assumes that the hypothesis is being tested using a two-tail test of the null hypothesis that β equals zero. That is, the program determines the t ratio, t_r, and then determines the aggregate area under the t distribution to the right of the positive value of t_r and the area to the left of the negative value of t_r.

An informal rule of thumb that is commonly used to quickly determine if the null hypothesis can be rejected is the "rule of 2." You will notice in the t table in Appendix B that with $df > 60$, the value of t in the table column headed 2.5% is less than 2. For two-tail tests of hypotheses at the 5% level of significance, this will be the critical value of the t ratio that is required to reject the null. So if a reader sees a t ratio greater than 2 when the degrees of freedom exceed 60, she can quickly conclude that the null that $\beta = 0$ can be rejected at the 5% level of significance.

F Statistic

In the case of multiple regression analysis, there are instances when one might wish to test hypotheses about all or some subset of the regression coefficients considered simultaneously. This is especially true if the investigator finds that it is not possible to reject the null hypothesis that individual coefficients on the independent variables differ from zero, yet has reason to believe that, taken simultaneously, the independent variables significantly affect the dependent variable.

In multiple regression analysis an investigator anticipates that each of the independent variables included in the equation will influence the dependent variable. It is of course possible that none of the independent variables are statistically significantly related to the dependent variable. More explicitly, if there were two independent variables in the equation but, using the above techniques, neither was found to be significantly different from zero at acceptable levels of significance, we could reject neither $H_0:\beta_1 = 0$ nor $H_0:\beta_2 = 0$.

Independently testing the two null hypotheses $H_0:\beta_1 = 0$ and $H_0:\beta_2 = 0$ is not the same thing as testing the null hypothesis that $H_0:\beta_1 = \beta_2 = 0$. The latter is a test of whether all of the coefficients taken together are simultaneously equal to zero, while the former tests whether each individually is equal to zero. In regression analysis it is possible not to reject the hypothesis that the coefficients individually are zero while at the same time rejecting the hypothesis that simultaneously the coefficients are all zero. To fail to reject the null hypothesis that simultaneously the coefficients are zero means that there is reason to believe that the entire model is not statistically significant. The test for the simultaneous equality of all regression coefficients (or some subset thereof) equaling zero is done through the use of the *F statistic.*

One might wonder how it is possible to reject the null hypothesis $H_0:\beta_1 = \beta_2 = 0$ when it is not possible to reject either the null hypothesis $H_0:\beta_1 = 0$ or the null hypothesis $H_0:\beta_2 = 0$. As one explanation, consider the following example: Suppose that in our food expenditure example we had used family size and the number of children (under the age of 21) as the only two independent variables. These two variables are highly correlated.[9] As will be seen in Chapter 5 in the discussion of multicollinearity, when two independent variables are correlated, the estimated standard errors of the regression coefficients are larger than they would be in the absence of one or the other correlated independent variable. Thus, because of large standard errors we may be unable to reject the two null hypotheses $H_0:\beta_1 = 0$ and $H_0:\beta_2 = 0$. Instead of testing each coefficient separately, we could instead test whether taken together the two independent variables affect food consumption. In the food expenditure example, the null hypothesis $H_0:\beta_1 = \beta_2 = 0$ is expected to be rejected in favor of the alternate hypothesis that one or the other (or both) of the independent variables is different from zero.

Just as hypothesis testing regarding a single regression coefficient depends on the sample data and the Student's t distribution, the F statistic relies on the sample data and a probability distribution called the *F distribution.* Use and interpretation of the F statistic are similar to those of the t statistic. Just as a t ratio can be computed to aid in hypothesis testing, an F statistic can also be constructed and compared to an *F* value obtainable from a table published in most statistics books. (See Appendix D for a list of such books.)

---

[9]They are highly correlated because family size is normally equal to the number of children plus one or two adults.

If the F statistic is greater than the critical value of the F found in the table, one can reject the null hypothesis that the regression coefficients taken in combination are equal to zero. In the food expenditure regression example which uses income and family size as explanatory variables (equation 2.3), the value of the F statistic is 37.98, while the F critical value is 3.19 for the 5% level of significance with degrees of freedom of (2, 47). (The degrees of freedom are expressed as two numbers separated by a comma. The first represents the number of coefficients being tested simultaneously, while the second is the number of observations used in the regression minus the number of regression coefficients estimated in the multiple regression.) One can thus reject the null hypothesis that $\beta_1 = \beta_2 = 0$ at the 5% level of significance, since $37.98 > 3.19$.[10]

The F statistic is related to the degree of explanatory power of the entire regression equation, since it is equal to

$$\text{F statistic} = \left(\frac{R^2}{\left(1 - R^2\right)} \right)\left(\frac{n - k - 1}{k} \right) \qquad [3.5]$$

where n is the number of observations and k is the number of independent variables in the regression (excluding the intercept term). This is why some researchers include a statement indicating if the R^2 is statistically significant or not.

What Tests of Significance Can and Cannot Do

Before turning to Chapter 4, it is important to emphasize the strengths and limitations of the hypothesis-testing procedure. Its strength is that in the presence of randomness, the procedure allows us to draw inferences about the population parameter. Since any estimate of a population parameter is likely to have some random component, this is a substantial benefit. In this analysis we have stressed randomness due to sampling, but other sources of randomness also exist. For example, measurement error (discussed in Chapter 5) could lead to some randomness even if one had information on the entire population.

The weakness of the method is that researchers may forget what exactly it is they have tested. Finding that a coefficient is statistically significantly

---

[10]F statistics can also be used to test the statistical significance of combinations of parameters when three or more variables are included in the regression. As is illustrated in Appendix C, the results of F tests in computer-based statistical packages are often shown under the heading of "Analysis of Variance" (sometimes termed *ANOVA*).

different from zero does not imply that the corresponding variable is necessarily important. Remember, statistical significance does not necessarily imply political, social, economic, or practical significance. The relationship found may be so small—even though statistically significant—that the variable is of little consequence. For example, suppose a study shows that a tax on sugared beverages has a statistically significant effect on the consumption of such beverages. If the results suggest that a 5-cent tax would reduce consumption by one can of soda per person per year, you would probably not be impressed with the implications of the results. But if the results showed a reduction in consumption of 25 cans, you probably would.[11] The distinction between statistical significance and other types of significance, be they political, social, or economic, is particularly important to remember when estimates are based on large data sets that nearly always yield coefficients that are statistically significant.

Summary

Linear regression analysis provides a methodology for estimating the relationship between a dependent variable and one or more independent variables. In virtually all instances, the data upon which the estimates are based constitute a random sample from the population. The coefficients that the linear regression analysis produces are thus estimates of the unobserved population parameters. Hypothesis testing provides a method for making inferences about the unobserved population parameter from estimates of the parameter. The hypothesis testing procedure formulates a null hypothesis and its opposite, called the alternate hypothesis. The procedure then draws on statistical theory to make inferences, at a chosen level of probability, as to whether the null hypothesis can be rejected in favor of the alternate hypothesis. Coefficients are said to be statistically significant in instances where the null hypothesis can be rejected in favor of the alternate at the specified probability.

   Closely related techniques are used, as well, to construct confidence intervals around estimated coefficients. In the case of multiple linear regression, additional hypothesis tests can be performed on sets of the regression coefficients.

---

[11]For a discussion of the limitations of tests of significance, see McCloskey (1985).

CHAPTER 4. EXTENSIONS TO
THE MULTIPLE REGRESSION MODEL

Introduction

The first two chapters present the rudiments of simple and multiple linear regression. Chapter three illustrates how the results from such analysis can be used to test hypotheses. This chapter explores a variety of ways regression analysis is extended beyond the basic models explained in the previous chapters. We begin by illustrating the various types of data that can be and are used in regression analysis. We then introduce and explain so-called dummy variables that are used in many published studies. Another technique that makes regression a powerful analytical tool is the use of various transformations of independent and dependent variables, which allow nonlinear relationships between variables to be studied within linear regression analysis. Finally we illustrate how regression analysis can be used to make predictions of dependent variables, with the chapter closing with four additional examples of published studies utilizing regression techniques.

Types of Data

The data used in the food consumption example are known as *cross-sectional data*, since they have been generated by a slice or cross section of the population at the same point in time. A second important data form is *time series data*, in which variables are measured at different points in time. Annual or quarterly gross domestic product (GDP) data and national divorce rates for the past 30 years each constitute time series data sets.

Regression estimation techniques and interpretation of the results are exactly the same for time series data as for cross-sectional data. Consider, for example, a study of the relationship across time between imports into the United States and the level of GDP. One might hypothesize that imports into a country during a year are positively related to the country's GDP in that year. If the relationship is assumed to be linear, it can be written as

$$M_t = \alpha + \beta \, GDP_t \qquad [4.1]$$

where M_t denotes the dollar value of imports observed in year t and GDP_t represents the level of GDP during that same year. Using the techniques discussed in previous chapters, historical values of M and GDP can be used to estimate α and β.

When studying behavior over time, it is sometimes hypothesized that the value of a variable in one time period is dependent on its value in the previous period. This is reasonable if behavior is conditioned by habits that persist over time. In such cases the previous period's value of the dependent variable can be used as an independent variable, and is called a *lagged dependent variable*. For example, in the previous problem one might specify that imports in year t depend on both the level of GDP in year t and on the level of M in year $t-1$. That is,

$$M_t = \alpha + \beta_1 GDP_t + \beta_2 M_{t-1} \qquad [4.2]$$

Similarly, there are situations in which it is more appropriate to use the previous period's value of the independent variable. For example, the yield from some agricultural products in one month may be dependent on rainfall in the current month as well as in previous months.

A more complex form of data can be created when cross-sectional information is combined over time to form *panel data* sets (sometimes referred to as *longitudinal data*). Observations on a set of families over time or financial data collected from a sample of counties in the United States observed for several years would each constitute panel data, as would observations on a set of students during their years of study. While statistical procedures needed to carry out such an analysis are more complex than the procedure outlined earlier, the underlying principles still hold.[1]

In addition to their time dimension, data can also be classified according to the degree of aggregation across behavioral units. *Micro data* measure characteristics of units of a population, such as individuals, families, or firms; *aggregate data* measure behavior for a group of such units.[2] A sample of 2015 GDP data for a set of countries forms a cross section of aggregate data, while the GDP for Mexico during the period 1980–2015 constitutes a time series of aggregate information. The food consumption example consists of micro cross-sectional data; if one observed wheat sales of an individual farm for the period 1980–2015, the resulting data set would constitute micro time series data. The form of the data does not, in general, alter the procedures nor the interpretation of results. Certain of the statistical problems discussed in Chapter 5 are, however, more frequently associated with the particular form of the data.

The value of the R^2 statistics obtained from different types of data are likely to differ. First, since behavior is often conditioned by past actions, there is generally less randomness when a unit is observed over time than when a cross section of units is studied. For example, the amount of driving

---

[1]The study of the relationship between volunteerism and foreclosure rates summarized in Chapter 2 uses panel data.

[2]The distinction between aggregate and micro data is somewhat artificial. For example, families consisting of more than one member can be considered aggregate units, and a firm's sales are probably due to the combined efforts of several persons. Nevertheless, it is important when observing regression results to recognize the degree of aggregation implied by the data.

you do this year is probably not too different from the amount you did last year. On the other hand, if one were to observe miles driven for a cross section of individuals, the data set might contain salesmen who travel for a living and retired persons who drive primarily to go grocery shopping. Because it is challenging to control for all the variation that occurs in a cross section of individuals, one will generally find higher R^2 values with time series data than with cross-sectional information.

Second, aggregate data from many firms or households hide certain differences in behavior among these units, since "high" and "low" values cancel each other out. This "averaging" means that there is less variability in the dependent variable to be explained by the independent variable(s) and often results in higher R^2 values for the aggregate information than for comparable micro data.

These possible differences in the variability of the data constitute a major reason that you should not simply look at the R^2 results of studies and praise those in which the R^2 is high while scoffing at those with low R^2 values. It is quite possible for all regression coefficients to be significantly different from zero, and yet for the coefficient of determination to be very small. If testing hypotheses about the regression coefficients is the aim of the study, the coefficient of determination should be considered only as additional information, not as the summary indicator of the quality of results.

Dummy Variables

Most of the independent variables discussed thus far are *continuous variables*, since they can generally assume an infinite number of values or integer values such as family size that, at least in principle, have no upper bound. Often, however, *dummy independent variables* are employed in regression analysis. Such variables, sometimes called *categorical, dichotomous,* or *binary variables*, take on only the values of 0 or 1. The use of such a variable is appropriate whenever the theory implies that behavior differs between two different time periods (e.g., during Republican and Democratic administrations), or between two groups within a cross section (e.g., married and unmarried individuals). Dummy variables can also be used in evaluating the efficacy of a treatment to indicate whether a subject is in the experimental or control group.[3]

In the food consumption problem, theory may lead one to hypothesize that the purchase of food differs between families who have gardens and grow some of their own fruits and vegetables and families without such gardens. The independent variable G can then be added to the regression equation where G takes the value of 1 if the spending unit maintains a garden and 0 if it does not (Table 1.1, column 4). Assume that one is interested only in the effects of income, I, and gardening status, G, on C. Estimates of the

---

[3]A more extensive treatment of the use of dummy variables can be found in Hardy (1993).

56

parameters can be derived using the techniques of multiple linear regression analysis. The results from such an analysis are

$$C = 4447.82 + 0.063I - 746.05G \qquad [4.3]$$

The coefficient on G indicates that, based on the sample, food expenditures for families with gardens are estimated to be \$746.05 less than those for families without a garden but *who have the same income*. This can be seen by substituting the two possible values of G (0 and 1) into the estimated equation. For families with gardens ($G = 1$), the resulting equation is simply $4447.82 + 0.063I - 746.05$ (or \$3,701.77 + 0.063I).[4] The estimated relationships in Figure 4.1 illustrate that garden and nongarden groups are *assumed* to respond in the same way to changes in income. That is, the regression lines have identical slopes, but the intercept term for families with gardens lies \$746.05 below that for families without gardens.[5] See Box 4.1 for a discussion of the statistical significance of these findings.

Box 4.1   Statistical Significance of Coefficient on Gardening

The coefficient in equation 4.3 on the dummy variable G that represents families with a garden is -746.05. Its standard error is 979.51, which yields a t ratio of -0.76 with 47 degrees of freedom. If you were to test the two-tail null hypothesis H_o: $\beta_G = 0$ versus the alternate that it is not zero, this very small t ratio would lead you to *not* reject the null at a 0.10 level of significance, since the p-value is 0.45.

In such cases, authors often state that the variable has no statistically significant effect on the dependent variable or, more simply, that the variable is not significant.

One other point to note is that the adjusted R^2, that is, $\bar{R}^2$, is 0.562 when only income is used to explain variations in spending on food; when the variable G is added to the equation, the adjusted R^2 *falls* to 0.558 (although the unadjusted R^2 increases from 0.571 to 0.576). The fall in adjusted R^2 is commonly considered a reason not to include the additional variable in the analysis, although, ultimately, whether or not a variable should be included ought to depend on theory.

---

[4]This is why dummy variables are coded zero-one rather than some other numerical combination. The estimated coefficient on the dummy variable directly indicates the size of the effect on the dependent variable of the dummy category coded as one.

[5]Note that there would be no change in the implications of the results had the dummy variable G been defined to equal 1 for families without gardens and 0 for those with gardens. The estimated equation would have been $C = 3701.77 + 0.063I + 746.05G$. That is, the estimated response to the one-dollar increase in income would still be 0.063, and families without gardens (where $G = 1$) would still be shown to spend \$746.05 more on food than families with gardens but with equal income.

Figure 4.1 Garden and Nongarden Regression Lines

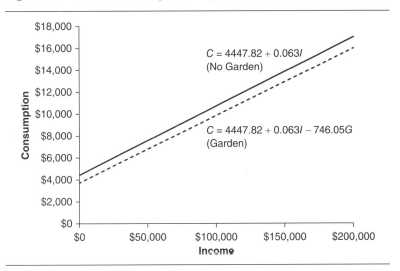

At times there may be more than two mutually exclusive categories that a variable can assume. For example, the race/ethnicity of a survey respondent may be classified as white, African American, Hispanic, or "other." (The race/ethnicity variable is an example of a nominal scale variable. See Box 4.2.) Again, dummy variables may be used to capture possible differences in the dependent variable across these groups or time periods.[6]

In such situations, *all but one* of the possible groupings of the classification variable are used as dummy variables. Thus, in the four-way grouping on race/ethnicity, three different dummy variables would be formed; one group is "excluded" and serves as a reference group against which comparisons can be made. It does not matter which group is chosen as the reference group; the implications of the results will remain the same. For example, if whites are chosen as the reference group, then three different dummy variables—African American, Hispanic, and other—would be formed. The variable "African American" would be equal to 1 only if the respondent were African American, otherwise, it would be 0. The variable "Hispanic" would be equal to 1 if the respondent were Hispanic, 0 otherwise, and similarly for the "other" group.[7]

---

[6]The reader should note that any continuous variable can be transformed into a classification variable. For example, while age is a continuous variable, surveys often report ages according to groups (e.g., less than 20 years of age, 20–65, or older than 65). The present discussion applies in those instances as well.

[7]The estimate for the excluded group is contained in the constant. Thus, in this example the constant term is an estimate of the value of Y for whites when X is zero. In the food consumption model, the constant term estimates what food consumption would be for individuals who do not have a garden and have no income.

The resulting equation of the dependent variable Y regressed against one continuous independent variable X and these dummy variables representing the race/ethnicity groups would be

$$Y = \alpha + \beta_1 X + \beta_2 African\ American + \beta_3 Hispanic + \beta_4 Other \qquad [4.4]$$

Multiple linear regression analysis would yield coefficient estimates on each of the included dummy variables. The intercept term captures the value of the dependent variable for the excluded reference group when the independent variable X has a zero value. The coefficient on each of the dummy variables is the estimate of the difference in the value of the dependent variable between the group in question and the excluded reference group. Thus the coefficient on "Hispanic" would estimate the difference in the dependent variable between Hispanics and whites (the reference group). The t ratio associated with the coefficient on a particular dummy variable can be used to test whether or not that group differs statistically from the reference group.

Categorical variables can also be created to represent different levels of a variable for which the exact value of the variable is not available. For example, education is sometimes categorized as less than a high school degree, only a high school degree, some college but no degree, et cetera. In this case dummy variables can be created for these various groups with one group, for example, no high school degree, serving as the reference group. Then the estimated coefficients on these dummy variables can be interpreted to represent the difference in the value of the dependent variable for each group relative to those without a high school degree.

Dummy variables are often used in analyzing panel data sets. For example, assume one would like to estimate the relationship between earnings and the number of years of education for a sample of 500 individuals observed over 20 years. The panel data set in this instance has 10,000 observations, 20 observations for each of the 500 individuals. We expect some of the variation in earnings to be due to unmeasurable factors that change from year to year. To control for these unmeasurable factors, we create dummy variables for each of 19 years and estimate the regression equation including these dummy variables. This is often referred to as a *fixed effects model*. We could also control for unmeasurable characteristics of the individuals by creating dummy variables for 499 of the individuals and estimate the equation between earnings and education with these 499 dummy variables, or controls. The coefficients on the dummy variables are generally not reported; instead, the regression is reported to have controlled for fixed effects or individual effects.

Interaction Variables

Another extension of the linear regression model occurs when *interaction effects* are included in an analysis. Three common types are interactions between a continuous variable and a dummy variable, interaction between two continuous variables, and interactions between two dummy variables.

Dummy Interaction Effects

The food consumption equation used earlier assumed that as income increases by one dollar, food consumption spending for both gardening and nongardening families increases in an identical fashion (by 6.3 cents). However, this may not always be a reasonable assumption. Dummy interaction variables allow an investigator to posit that the response to a change in a continuous independent variable differs between classified groups.

Consider again the food consumption example with income and garden/nongarden status as independent variables. A dummy interaction term yields the model

$$C = \alpha + \beta_1 I + \beta_2 G + \beta_3 IG \qquad [4.5]$$

where IG is the product of income (I) and G, the dummy variable for gardening.

The coefficient β_1 estimates the effect of a one-dollar change in income on food consumption for nongardeners, while for gardeners the estimated effect of income is $\beta_1 + \beta_3$, since $G = 1$ for this group. The estimate of β_3 would therefore be the differential effect of a one-dollar change in income on food expenditures between gardening and non-gardening families. Using the same data but including an interaction term between the dummy variable G (gardeners vs. nongardeners) and the continuous variable I yields the following regression results:

$$C = 4562.66 + 0.062I - 1257.29G + 0.008IG \qquad [4.6]$$

The implied graphical relationship between C and I is shown in Figure 4.2. Note that unlike the lines in Figure 4.1, the regression lines are not parallel when an interaction effect is included.

Interaction Effects Between Two Continuous Variables

There are also instances in which analysts expect that two continuous variables interact in their influence on a dependent variable. One example of such an interaction between two continuous variables is the ability to operate a motor vehicle when under the influence of alcohol and/or another legal or illegal drug. A dependent variable that measures ability could be reaction time. We would expect both additional amounts of alcohol consumed and additional consumption of the drug to be associated with slower reaction time. However, we also expect an interaction effect. If a subject has, for example, a 0.02 blood alcohol level, consumption of an additional amount of the drug can exacerbate the slower reaction time associated with that level of blood alcohol.

60

Figure 4.2   Gardening and Nongardening Regression Lines Allowing for Interaction

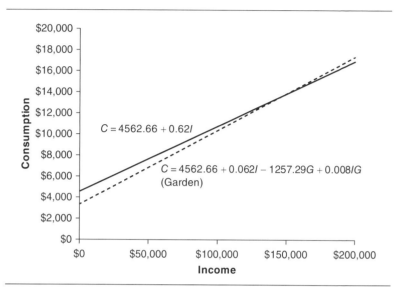

$$C = 4562.66 + 0.62I$$

$$C = 4562.66 + 0.062I - 1257.29G + 0.008IG$$
(Garden)

Box 4.2   Categorical and Ordinal Scale Variables

Numbers are sometimes used simply to represent different categories associated with a variable, such as 1, 2, 3, 4, in order to indicate, for example, which of the four regions of the United States—Northeast, Midwest, South, or West—a survey respondent resides in. These variables are called *nominal scale variables* since they represent different names with no ordering or ranking implied. Dummy variables discussed in this section are a type of nominal scale variable.

Ordinal scale variables are sometimes used in regression analysis. Such variables are meant to represent a hierarchical ordering and are often used to indicate levels of subjective "feelings" such as "very dissatisfied," "somewhat dissatisfied," "somewhat satisfied," or "very satisfied," which might be coded 1 through 4. One issue associated with such ordinal scale variables is that there may be no reason to assume that a one-unit change in the scale, for example, from 1 to 2, is conceptually equal to the change from 2 to 3 or from 3 to 4. Alternatively, dummy variables (0 or 1) can be assigned to each of these levels without assuming equal changes in intensity when moving from "very" to "somewhat" et cetera.

One of the ordinal scale variables often used in the social sciences is known as the *Likert Scale,* which is commonly used by researchers to measure attitudes. Likert scales (named after their originator, Rensis Likert) are constructed from questions that require the respondent to state his or her level of agreement or disagreement with a statement where the potential responses range from strong disagreement to strong agreement. Generally either five or seven levels of agreement are solicited from the respondent, for example, -3, -2, -1, 0, 1, 2, or 3, representing very strongly disagree, strongly disagree, disagree, neither agree or disagree, agree, strongly agree, or very strongly agree. Example 4.3 uses a seven-level scale as a dependent variable.

Interaction Effects Between Two Dummy Variables

There are also instances where two categorical variables may be hypothesized to interact. For instance, in an experimental setting a researcher might anticipate that the effects of an experiment vis-à-vis a control group will differ depending on the gender of the participant. For example, one might expect a different effect by gender of a program that provides childcare training for single parents. If Y is the measure of the outcome of the experiment and two categorical variables F (coded 1 for a female participant and 0 for a male) and T (coded 1 for a participant in the treatment group and 0 for the control group), and where FT is the product of F and T, the following regression equation could be estimated:

$$Y = a + b_1 F + b_2 T + b_3 \left(FT \right) \qquad [4.7]$$

There are four possible combinations of categories—females in the treatment group, males in the treatment group, females in the control group, and males in the control group. The estimate of the intercept term, a, represents the mean of Y for the group simultaneously coded 0, that is, males in the control group, and serves as the reference group against which the other groups are compared. The estimate of the coefficient on the interaction term, b_3, is the effect on Y for females in the treatment group. The estimates of b_1 and b_2 represent, respectively, the differential effect on Y of females in the control group (vis-à-vis the reference group) and males in the treatment group.

Transformations

The case of interaction terms is one example in which an independent variable has been *transformed*. Since linear regression worked well in that instance, it should not be surprising to find that other types of transformations can also be used. Probably the most common form of transformation is one that converts a nonlinear relationship between variables into a linear one. This is particularly important since it is generally recognized that not all relationships between variables are linear. At the same time, *linear* regression techniques are applicable when, as illustrated below, nonlinear relationships are transformed to create a linear equation using the transformed variable.

Students of economics are probably familiar with "U-shaped" average cost curves that imply that the cost of producing a unit of output declines at low levels of output and subsequently begins to rise at higher levels. The resulting plot of average costs on the vertical axis and output on the horizontal axis is a graph that takes the general shape of a U. In a somewhat similar example, if a country's population growth rate is 2% a year, a plot of population against time will result in a curve that rises nonlinearly. Since the 2% increase in population is being applied to a larger and larger base, as time passes larger absolute annual increases in population will result. Fortunately, in many such situations linear regression analysis can be used by transforming the nonlinear relationship into an equivalent, but linear, form.

Suppose that two variables, L and M, are theorized to be related in the following nonlinear manner:

$$L = \alpha' M^{\beta} \qquad [4.8]$$

where α' and β are two unknown parameters.[8] It is possible to rewrite equation 4.8 in a linear form by taking the natural logarithm (abbreviated *ln*) of both sides of the equality. This yields[9]

$$\ln L = ln\alpha' + \beta lnM. \qquad [4.9]$$

By redefining the terms in equation 4.9 as $Y = lnL$, $\alpha = ln\alpha'$, and $X = lnM$, equation 4.9 can be expressed as

$$Y = \alpha + \beta X \qquad [4.10]$$

Since this equation is identical to the simple linear regression equation 1.1 in Chapter 1, the techniques discussed there will yield estimates of α and β as well as their associated statistics. If the estimated value of β in equation 4.10 is found, for example, to be -1.2, the implication is that a one-unit increase in the *natural logarithm* of M is associated with a 1.2-unit decrease

---

[8]If, for example, $\alpha' = 1$ and $\beta = 2$, the resulting equation would be $L = M^2$. The reader should experiment with different values of M to verify that L and M are related nonlinearly as long as $\beta \neq 1$.

[9]Equation 4.9 relies on the following characteristics of mathematical operations on logarithms: $log (XY) = log (X) + log (Y)$, and $log (X^c) = c\ log (X)$ where X and Y are any two positive real numbers and c is a real number. The symbol ln denotes the special case of a logarithm to the base e.

in the *natural logarithm* of L. Another interpretation of the coefficient −1.2 is that for each 1% increase in M there is an associated 1.2% decrease in L.[10] Another method of handling nonlinear relationships with linear regression is by squaring an independent variable. The resulting relationship is termed a *polynomial model*, since it results in the following polynomial equation

$$Y = \alpha + \beta_1 X + \beta_2 X^2 \qquad [4.11]$$

This is a particularly interesting form of a nonlinear relationship, since it suggests that the change in Y for each unit change in X depends on the value of X.[11] Such a model can be used if an analyst believes, for example, that the effect of age on a dependent variable declines as the respondent ages (or initially increases and then declines). Likewise, equation 4.11 can trace out U- or inverted U-shaped relationships between an independent and dependent variable. This function could be used, for example, if an analyst expected housing rents to increase as one moved away from the congestion of the central business district (CBD), but at some distance away from the CBD, rents might begin to decline due to the costs of the long commute to work. Higher-order polynomial functions can be estimated in a similar manner.

Prediction

Besides testing hypotheses, linear regression results can also be used for purposes of predicting the value of a dependent variable for particular values of the independent variable(s). For the food consumption example, the result of a multiple linear regression using the three independent variables—income, family size, and the gardening dummy variable—is

$$C = 3179.40 + 0.054I + 803.61S - 470.26G \qquad [4.12]$$

Equation 4.12 can be used for prediction. For example, for a family of four without a garden and with an income of $50,000, the prediction would be $9,093.84 (= 3,179.40 + (0.054)(50,000) + (803.61)(4)).

Although regression results can be used for purposes of prediction, in certain instances regression findings may not be particularly useful for predicting values of the dependent variable, even though the results indicate that the variables

---

[10]Students of economics will recognize that the ratio of the percentage change in L relative to a percentage change in M is the definition of the elasticity of L with respect to M. Thus this transformation provides a convenient way to estimate elasticity coefficients. Note, too, that in this case the assumption is made that the elasticity is the same at all points along the relationship.

[11]From the calculus we know that $dY/dX = \beta_1 + 2\beta_2 X$; that is, the change in Y associated with a change in X depends on β_1, β_2, and X.

are significantly related to a dependent variable. This is particularly the case if the variables explain a small amount of the variation—indicated by a small R^2—which suggests that numerous other unmeasured or random factors also influence the size of the dependent variable.[12] In such instances it is heroic to predict particular values of the dependent variable on the basis of such results. Likewise, if the t ratios for the regression coefficients are quite low, one cannot have much confidence in the predicted results, since a low t ratio implies considerable uncertainty about the true population regression coefficient.[13]

Since the regression coefficients are estimated from a single set of data, one should also be suspicious of predictions based on extreme extrapolations from those data. For example, while one might use the food consumption results to predict Canadian food consumption, one would be ill advised to predict behavior in a very low income country with these results. Likewise, predictions for the year 2050 based on data collected over the period 1990–2015 may prove to be extremely inaccurate.

An additional aspect of using regression results for forecasting is that it may require predicting values for the independent variables. Errors in estimating the values of these variables for the future will result in forecasting errors for the dependent variable, even if the model itself is perfect.

Examples

A wide variety of applications of multiple linear regression using different types of data and alternative forms of variables are available in the literature. Here we consider only four to demonstrate this range of applicability. Bear in mind that the examples are not summaries of the articles, which commonly employ more extensive empirical analyses than what is presented here.

Example 4.1 The Effect of the Nobel Prize on Academic Citations

One measure of the influence of a professor's research is the extent to which that research is cited by others in the academic literature. Citations are generally assumed to reflect both the quality of the research as well as the reputation of the author being cited. One interesting study of citation analysis examines the effect of winning the Nobel Prize in Economics[14] on the number of citations, as measured by the Social Science Citation Index.

---

[12]Note that this is a situation where the size of the R^2 coefficient is of interest. There are, however, no generally accepted rules of thumb regarding how large the R^2 ought to be for forecasting.

[13]Just as confidence intervals can be constructed around estimated regression coefficients, prediction intervals can be constructed around predicted values of the dependent variable, again with prespecified levels of confidence in the predictions (with higher levels of confidence associated with wider prediction intervals).

[14]The formal name of the prize is "The Sveriges Riksbank Prize in Economic Sciences in Memory of Alfred Nobel."

The study by Landes and Lahr-Pastor (2011) uses time trend analysis along with a dummy variable set equal to one in each of the years following the awarding of the prize. Although the citations of various award winners are analyzed using regression analysis, we focus here on the results for Ronald Coase, who was awarded the prize in 1991. As the dependent variable the authors use the natural logarithm of the number of citations (*ln C*) of Coase's work for each year between 1960 and 2008. Their independent variables are time in years ($T = 1, 2, \ldots, 49$) and time (years) squared (T^2) (to allow the trend to either slow or increase as time passes) along with the dummy variable *Nobel*, which is set equal to 0 up until the year the prize was awarded, and to 1 thereafter. The resulting regression equation (with all coefficients significant at the 0.001 level of significance and an R^2 of 0.96) is

$$lnC = 0.844 + 0.208T - 0.002T^2 + 0.315Nobel \qquad [4.13]$$

The results indicate that the citations increased in the early years at an approximately 20% rate (remember that changes in the natural log of the dependent variable can be interpreted as percentage changes) but that as time went on that rate of increase was slowing. Finally, winning the Nobel was followed by a substantial increase in the number of citations.

Example 4.2 The Effect of Copyright Laws on the Composition of Operas

Proponents of copyright laws argue that such laws promote creativity by providing incentives for composers and authors to gain financially from their efforts. A test of the relationship between output of composers and the introduction of copyright laws was done by Giorcelli and Moser (2015). The authors' analysis takes advantage of the fact that after the invasion by Napoleon's army in 1800, the Italian provinces of Lombardy and Venetia adopted French copyright law in 1801. To test their hypothesis, the authors collected annual data on the number of operas that premiered in each of eight Italian states over the period 1770 to 1900. They use the number of opera premieres per state per year as the dependent variable and create the dummy variable "Province of Lombardy or Venetia x Post 1801" to control for the extension of copyright laws to these two provinces. (The variable is the interaction of two dummy variables: one dummy measures whether the premieres were in Lombardy or Venetia, and the other dummy measures premieres that occurred post 1801.) The authors also control for fixed effects for each of the provinces of Italy as well as fixed effects for each year. The coefficient on the interaction variable is 2.124, indicating that post 1801 there were 2.124 more premieres per year in Lombardy and Venetia than in other Italian states, suggesting that the use of copyrights had a positive effect on the number of new opera productions. The coefficient is significant at the 0.001 level

Example 4.3 Effects of Attitudes Toward
Immigration on Political Partisianship

A major policy issue in the United States in the early 21st century has been immigration, with the public having a wide range of views concerning its desirability. Hajnal and Rivera (2014) address the question of how the perceptions of white voters in the United States affect their political party preferences. Specifically, the authors hypothesize that white voters with stronger negative views regarding immigration identify more strongly with the Republican Party. To test the hypothesis, they rely on opinion survey research conducted by the American National Election Study during the 2008 presidential campaign, when immigration was not a particularly important issue. The data used are restricted to survey respondents who are white and non-Hispanic. The dependent variable is a scale indicating political party preference ranging from 1 (strongly Democratic) to 7 (strongly Republican). The authors construct an indicator that reflects survey respondents' positive views toward immigrants based on the respondents' answers to four different questions regarding immigration and immigrants.[15] That variable and several additional demographic variables that are expected to influence individuals' politically partisan attitudes were used to analyze political party identification. The results are shown in Table 4.1 and support the authors' hypothesis that individuals with stronger positive views toward illegal immigrants are less likely to identify with the Republican Party, even after taking into account other personal characteristics that are likely to affect political party identification.[16] The coefficient on the "Views" variable is significant at the 0.005 level.

Example 4.4 Sales of Lightweight Vehicles

During the 2008–2009 Great Recession, the US government engaged in the highly controversial policy of helping to rescue the US automobile industry. As part of an evaluation of this bailout, Goolsbee and Krueger (2015) compare actual car sales post–Great Recession to car sales predicted by a forecasting model. The forecasting model takes the form of a time series regression equation that uses several variables to explain quarterly sales of lightweight vehicles for the period 1977 through 2007. Table 4.2 contains the regression results. Using the regression equation, they predict

---

[15]A statistical technique beyond the scope of this book called "factor analysis" was used to construct the scale, which the authors report ranged from −2.8 to +1.7.

[16]The article estimates other more complex models that include a variety of attitudinal variables that could affect party identification; nevertheless in each model the attitude toward illegal immigration remains statistically significant in support of the authors' research hypothesis.

Table 4.1 Identification as Republication and Views on Immigration
Among Whites

Independent Variable	Regression Coefficient	Standard Error
Positive views toward illegal immigration	−0.61	0.09
Education	−0.01	0.03
Income	0.04	0.01
Unemployed	0.16	0.33
Age	−0.08	0.04
Female	−0.20	0.14
Married	0.57	0.14
Union member	−0.53	0.21
Jewish	−1.30	0.52
Catholic	0.16	0.18
Protestant	0.80	0.16
Intercept	4.39	0.50
Number of observations	803	
Adjusted R^2	0.12	

Source: Adapted from Hajnal and Rivera (2014).

Table 4.2 Regression Model of Lightweight Vehicle Sales, 1977–2007

Variables	Regression Coefficient	Standard Error
Real GDP growth (%)	0.099	0.025
Unemployment rate (%)	−1.150	0.093
Population growth (%)	0.226	0.116
SLOOS credit availability	0.044	0.009
Log gasoline price (lagged)	−0.027	0.808
Standard deviation of log gasoline price over previous four quarters	8.657	4.033
Constant	15.948	1.357
R^2	0.716	

Source: Adapted from Goolsbee and Krueger (2015)

68

annual sales in the post-2007 period and find that their predictions closely match actual sales, suggesting that sales in the post-2007 period were driven by the same factors as in the pre-2007 period.

The first three variables, inflation-adjusted gross domestic product (GDP) growth, the unemployment rate, and population growth, are hypothesized to affect the demand for lightweight vehicles. The SLOOS credit availability variable, which is the Federal Reserve's Senior Loan Officer Opinion Survey measure of the willingness to lend to consumers, reflects the ability to get financing for a car purchase. Gasoline is a significant cost of operating a car, so it is expected that higher gasoline prices are associated with fewer sales. Here the variable is entered in its log form and lagged one quarter, reflecting the idea that purchasing decisions are influenced by events in the recent past. Because the authors expected greater variability in gas prices to reduce car sales, they also included the standard deviation of the log of gasoline prices as an independent variable.

With the exception of the variability of gas prices, all coefficients have the signs the authors expected. And while the results suggest that higher gasoline prices have a negative effect on vehicle sales, the t ratio of only 0.033 indicates that the variable is not statistically significant.

These four examples illustrate the variety of subjects that are analyzed using various linear regression estimation techniques. The examples also show that researchers' theories or hypotheses are not always supported by the empirical evidence.

Summary

Linear regression analysis can be applied to a wide variety of types of data. In some instances the data are collected at one point in time (cross-sectional); in other instances data are collected over time. Sometimes multiple cross sections are combined, producing what is referred to as panel data. The ability to transform data by applying various mathematical operations means that the linear regression technique can be used to examine nonlinear relationships. Several examples of such nonlinear relationships have been provided in this chapter. The creation of what are referred to as "dummy" variables allows the analyst to examine whether behavior differs across groups of individuals, different periods of time, or different types of discrete treatment. The results from regression analyses can also be used to predict values of the dependent variable for various values of the independent variable(s). However, it is important for the reader to recognize that there are various statistical and methodological issues that accompany regression analysis. We turn to a brief examination of these in the final chapter.

CHAPTER 5. PROBLEMS AND ISSUES ASSOCIATED WITH REGRESSION

Introduction

Almost anyone who has a computer can estimate a linear regression. Regression analysis, for example, can easily be done using a basic spreadsheet program, such as Excel, or by use of any one of a number of statistical packages that are widely available. (Appendix C reproduces the output from estimating equation 1.2 using Excel and four commonly used statistical packages.) The use of such programs is reasonably easy. Although the preceding discussion may seem to suggest that regression analysis is a straightforward exercise without pitfalls, this unfortunately is not the case. Thus, a purely mechanical application of such packages is not appropriate.

Regression analysis, especially hypothesis testing, is based on several important assumptions. These include (1) that the correct equation is being used, that is, the proper variables are included as independent variables and the proper functional form is used; (2) that the variables are measured accurately; (3) that the independent variables are independent of each other; (4) that the data constitute a random sample; and (5) that the residual error term, as explained below, is "well-behaved." (Recall that the residual error term refers to the difference between the observed value of the dependent variable and its value as predicted from the estimated regression equation.) Difficulties arise in regression analysis when any of these assumptions are violated. Computer packages do not automatically solve these difficulties; it is up to the researcher to handle them.

This final chapter addresses some of the more common problems associated with linear regression, the implications each problem has on the results of the analysis, and some of the methods that analysts use to circumvent the difficulties. The objective is to make the reader aware of the issues, not to explain how to handle them, since that is beyond the scope of the book. We begin with the issue that every analyst faces—specification of the model. Next, we examine issues associated with variables used in the regression analysis and the measurement of these variables. We then discuss various problems related to the form of the error term in the regression equation. We conclude the chapter with a brief discussion of the topics of endogeneity and simultaneous equations, experiments, instrumental variables, and the case of a 0-1 dependent variable. Appendix D contains a list of books that discuss regression analysis. Most of these discuss the issues presented in this chapter in considerably more detail.

Specification of the Model

Although all of the issues discussed in this chapter are, loosely speaking, associated with specification, we limit ourselves to specification problems that analysts face when deciding which variables to include and exclude in a regression equation and the functional form of that equation. Unfortunately, omitting a relevant variable, including an irrelevant variable, or using an improper functional form can produce undesirable effects on the results.

Omitting a Relevant Variable

When a variable is omitted from a regression equation, the regression coefficients on the included variables will, in general, be unreliable or invalid, since they will be "biased" estimates of the true population regression coefficients. *Bias,* or the lack thereof, which is termed *unbiased*, is a theoretical statistical property associated with the estimation of unknown population parameters. An unbiased estimator will, on average, yield estimates equal to the (unknown) population parameter. Hence, being unbiased is considered a desirable property of an estimator.

In Chapter 3 we gave the example of estimating the mean height of a population of students in a large university. Statistical theory states that a sample mean taken from a random sample is an unbiased estimator of a population mean. This implies that if a large number of different random samples were drawn from the population of students, the *average* of those sample means would be equal to the population mean height. Note that even though the sample mean is an unbiased estimator, it does not imply that a single sample mean will be equal to the population mean. Statisticians have shown that if certain assumptions (noted below) hold, the estimators of regression coefficients discussed in Chapters 1 and 2 are unbiased estimators of the population coefficients.

The fact that omission of a relevant variable will lead to biased regression coefficient estimates is intuitively plausible. Suppose that two variables, income and family size, are the sole determinants of food consumption and that all other variability in food purchases across families is purely a random occurrence. If the analyst uses only income to explain variability in food consumption and if income and family size are correlated, the estimated coefficient on income will reflect the effects of both income and family size on food purchases.[1] This is why the addition of family size to the food consumption equation reduced the estimated effect of a $1 increase in income from 6.4 cents to 5.5 cents.

Since the task of regression analysis is to estimate the response in the dependent variable to changes in an independent variable, an incorrect

---

[1]If the independent variables are not correlated, then it doesn't matter if the other variable is included or not.

estimate of that response can be serious. Unfortunately, there is little an analyst can do to detect whether an important variable has been left out of the equation. Because of the uncertainty regarding omitted variables, researchers often include results from two or more different specifications of the same phenomenon. If, under alternative specifications, there is little change in the size of the estimated coefficients, the estimates are said to be *robust*. Such experimentation strengthens the analyst's belief in the model used; even so, one can never be absolutely certain that a relevant variable has not been omitted.

Inclusion of an Irrelevant Variable

One might think that, since omitting a relevant variable is "bad," the solution to the problem is to throw every possible variable into the equation. This solution also has pitfalls. If a variable is included in the equation but is not in fact relevant, the estimates of the coefficients will be unbiased. However, if the irrelevant variable is correlated with the included relevant variables, the size of the estimated standard errors of the coefficients of the relevant variables will increase (see the discussion of multicollinearity below). This in turn means that the t ratio will be smaller than if the correct specification were used. Hence, by including the irrelevant variable, the analyst is more likely to conclude that the coefficient on a relevant variable is not significantly different from zero (i.e., the researcher will not be able to reject the null hypothesis that there is no association with the dependent variable). Adding unnecessary variables can increase the standard errors; as such it causes a loss in precision of the estimated coefficients on the relevant variables.

Incorrect Functional Form

In the previous chapters it was shown that least squares linear regression is not restricted to simple linear relationships among variables. There are, in fact, myriad possible functional forms that are amenable to estimation using least squares techniques. The issue is which form to use.

If the underlying relationship between variables is not that of a straight line but a linear function is estimated, the resulting coefficient will be biased. Suppose you want to explore the effect on an exam score of the hours of study during the 24 hours prior to the exam. One might hypothesize that initially more study will increase the exam score, but at some point more hours of study (and the corresponding lack of sleep) will result in a lower exam score. If that were the true relationship, then the estimate of β using a straight line equation would be a misleading indicator of the functional relationship between hours of study and exam score.

One way in which nonlinearities may be detected is to plot the residual error terms (the difference between the actual value of the dependent variable and its value as estimated from the equation). If there are large negative (positive) residuals at low and high values of an independent variable and large positive (negative) residuals at intermediate levels of the independent variable, a nonlinear relationship is suggested.

Stepwise Regression

Since decisions regarding which of numerous possible variables to include in a regression equation are difficult, *stepwise regression* techniques are sometimes used. These techniques let the computer experiment with different combinations of independent variables.

In one method of stepwise regression, the computer first estimates simple linear regressions using each of all the possible independent variables specified by the analyst. For example, if there were 20 possible independent variables, the computer program would estimate 20 different simple linear regressions. From the set of 20 results the program would choose which one is "best." This selection, which is a part of the computer program, usually relies on the coefficient of multiple determination, R^2.

In step 2 the program would try each of the 19 remaining independent variables together with the variable chosen in step 1 and produce 19 different regression results, each with two independent variables. Again, the rule regarding which of these 19 is "best" would be invoked and results from this second step would be printed. This process continues until either all 20 variables are included in the equation or no remaining variable increases the R^2 statistic sufficiently to permit the inclusion of additional variables.

Although R^2 statistics can be tested using an F distribution (see equation 3.5 in Chapter 3), it should be recognized that changes in R^2 attributable to any particular variable usually depend on what variables are already in the equation. For example, when income alone is used in the food consumption example, the R^2 is 0.571. If family size is the sole regressor used to explain food spending, the R^2 is 0.292; adding income as a second regressor increases the R^2 to 0.618. This second approach would suggest that income explains only an additional 32.6% ($0.326 = 0.618 - 0.292$) of the total variability in food consumption, rather than 57.1% as indicated above. Incremental changes in R^2 values should therefore be interpreted in terms of which other variables have already been included in the model. Without careful thought, stepwise regression analysis can turn into a fishing expedition that is void of theory. It is therefore far better to rely on theory to construct your models. If that leads to multiple possible specifications, stepwise regression may be appropriate.

In summary, specification is a perplexing problem faced by most analysts. Misspecification can produce misleading or imprecise results. Furthermore, computational techniques relying heavily on computers and devoid of theory do not provide the solution. Innovative thought and theory are the most important ingredients in addressing problems of specification.

Variables Used in Regression Equations and Measurement of Variables

A number of issues arise that are associated with the variables used in regression analysis and the measurement of those variables. Three are discussed here.

Proxy Variables and Measurement Error

While theorizing about appropriate variables is not always easy, actually observing some variables and measuring them accurately can be equally difficult. The desired variables often are not available. In such cases analysts often turn to alternative, second-best measures of the phenomenon at hand. The variables chosen are termed *proxy variables* since they are used to approximate the real thing. The degree of approximation will influence the estimated impact of the variable of actual interest.

There are many examples of uses of proxy variables in the literature. Whenever dummy variables are substituted for what is really a continuous variable, a proxy is being used. For example, some analysts of political behavior may theorize that the "liberalism" of the president affects particular types of behavior. But, in the absence of a direct measure of liberal tendencies, they may use a dummy variable set equal to 1 if the president is a Democrat and 0 if a Republican or use some other approximation of political beliefs.

In other instances, variables that are readily available are substituted as a proxy for unobserved variables. For example, even though theory may suggest that work experience influences wages, years of experience may not be available in a data set. In such instances researchers often substitute age under the assumption that the older the worker, the greater his or her work history. This measure, or a derivative thereof (such as age minus the years of education less five to reflect years prior to starting school), may be reasonably accurate for workers with continuous labor market experiences. It is, however, less accurate in cases where individuals have had discontinuous labor market work histories.

Use of imperfect proxy variables can introduce errors of measurement into the analysis. Another form of measurement error is simply mismeasurement of the variables that are available. For example, some respondents to a survey may deliberately misstate their age or not report accurately the candidate for whom they voted. Measurement error can also occur if survey questions are asked in an ambiguous way.

Measurement errors can result in biased estimates of regression coefficients. Sometimes these errors can be avoided through more accurate data collection procedures; however, when analysts use data collected by others, it is unlikely that much can be done to improve the quality of the data. Instead, cognizance should be taken of the probable measurement errors and how systematic over- or underreporting of either the independent or dependent variables might influence the estimated coefficients.

Selection Bias

There are instances in which, even though every variable is measured accurately, the nature of the sample is such that the observations are for a nonrepresentative sample of the population. All results based on questionnaires that can be completed by anyone who is willing to put forth the effort are potentially nonrepresentative, since the participants have been self-selected. Similarly, when studying the factors that might explain differences in women's wages, women not in the labor force are excluded from the analysis. In such a case the results of the regression analysis cannot readily be used to predict the wage that a woman currently not working could get if she were to get a job. This is because there is likely some systematic difference between women who are working in the labor market and those who are not working for wages. Any regression based only on the former group will not capture this influence. If the regression results from the censored sample (working women) are to be used to make inferences about all women, it is necessary to adjust for the selection bias that exists.[2]

Multicollinearity

A final problem associated with variables used in multiple regression analysis is multicollinearity. It arises whenever two or more independent variables used in a regression are not independent but are correlated, thus violating one of the assumptions underlying linear regression analysis and hypothesis testing.

When two or more independent variables are highly correlated, the statistical estimation techniques discussed earlier are incapable of sorting out the independent effects of each on the dependent variable. For example, New York State imposed a mandatory seat belt law at about the same time that law enforcement agencies in the state cracked down on drunken drivers. For this reason, any subsequent decline in auto fatalities cannot be attributed exclusively to either one or the other of these policies.

Although the estimated coefficients using correlated independent variables are unbiased, they tend to have larger standard errors than they would

---

[2]The economist James Heckman shared the Nobel Prize in Economics in 2000 for work related to selection bias and ways to correct for it.

have in the absence of multicollinearity. This in turn means that the t ratios will be smaller. Thus, when multicollinearity plagues the data, it is more likely that one will find the regression coefficients not to be statistically significant than in the case where no multicollinearity is present. In essence, the presence of multicollinearity means that there is less precision associated with estimated coefficients.

Multicollinearity is probably present in almost all multiple regression analysis within the social sciences, since many socioeconomic variables such as education, social status, political preference, income, and wealth are likely to be interrelated. Time series data are also likely to exhibit multicollinearity, because many economic series tend to move in the same direction (e.g., production, income, and employment data). Whether multicollinearity is a problem depends on the degree of collinearity. The difficulty is that there is no one statistical test that can determine categorically if it is really a problem. One method of assessing whether multicollinearity is a problem is to look for "high" correlation coefficients between the independent variables included in a regression equation. Even then, however, this approach is not foolproof, since multicollinearity also exists if linear combinations of variables are used in a regression equation.[3] Another method, found in most statistical packages, estimates a measure called the variance inflation factor (VIF) that quantifies the degree to which the standard error of an independent variable is "inflated" because of multicollinearity with one or more other variables.

There is no single preferable technique for overcoming multicollinearity, since the problem is due to the form of the data. If two variables are measuring the same thing, however, one of the variables is often dropped, since little information is lost by doing so. However, one cannot claim that the effect on the dependent variable is due exclusively to the included variable, since the other variable could have been used instead. Thus, one has to acknowledge that the result could be due to either of the two variables. One way to approach such a situation is to use an F test to test the null hypothesis that neither of the variables is significantly related versus the null hypothesis that at least one is, although we can't say which one.

Violations of Assumptions Regarding Residual Errors

Proxy variables, measurement errors, selection bias, and multicollinearity all relate to the data available to a researcher. The next set of issues pertains to assumptions regarding the residual error term (see equation 1.2).

---

[3]Without proof, this is the reason that, when dummy variables representing three or more classes of outcomes are analyzed, one group is omitted from the analysis. Without such omission, perfect multicollinearity would exist between the three variables, and the equation could not be estimated.

The discussion of regression analysis in Chapters 1 and 2 is based on the *ordinary least squares* (OLS) *regression model*. The desirable statistical properties of the OLS model are based on four assumptions regarding the error terms, which is what we meant above when we stated that the residual errors needed to be "well behaved":

Assumption 1: even though some errors are small and others are large, some are positive and others are negative, they have a mean of zero;

Assumption 2: the error term associated with one observation is uncorrelated with the error term associated with all other observations;

Assumption 3: while some of the error terms may be small and others large, the variability of the error terms is in no way related to the independent variables used; and

Assumption 4: the error term is not correlated with the independent variables.

Violations of any of these assumptions produce undesirable statistical properties in the results obtained when regression coefficients are estimated without regard for these assumptions. While a full discussion of these topics is beyond our scope, it is useful to review the most common problems regarding residual errors that arise in the course of regression analysis and to indicate the steps that analysts take in response to these problems.

Autocorrelation

The term *autocorrelation*[4] refers to the case in which the residual errors from different observations are correlated. If the errors are positively correlated, *positive autocorrelation* is said to exist, while if they are negatively correlated, *negative autocorrelation* is present. Autocorrelation and the problems it presents are more likely to appear with time series data. Most commonly the problem is restricted to error terms associated with successive time periods, such that over (or under) estimates of the dependent variable in one period are correlated with over (or under) estimates in the following period. In the case of positive autocorrelation, a positive (negative) difference between the estimated value of the dependent variable and the actual value in one period (the error term for that period) is likely to be followed in the next period by another positive (negative) error term rather than a purely random error. In the case of negative autocorrelation, a positive error term in one period is very likely to be followed by a negative error term in the subsequent time period.

---

[4] Autocorrelation is sometimes referred to as serial correlation.

Autocorrelation can be caused by several factors, including omission of an important explanatory variable or the use of an incorrect functional form. It may also simply be due to the tendency of effects to persist over time or for variables to behave cyclically. For example, positive autocorrelation would occur if home sales were regressed on time given that there are years when home sales are considerably above the long-term time trend and other years when home sales fall short of that trend. Negative autocorrelation can occur if individuals adjust their behavior this period in light of what happened last period. By way of example, the amount of time a faculty member spends with a student during office hours may be negatively correlated with the amount of time the faculty member spent with the preceding student.

Whatever the cause, autocorrelation influences the outcome of the hypothesis-testing procedure. The effect of positive autocorrelation is underestimation of the standard error of the estimated coefficient, s_b. This in turn yields an inflated t ratio, which means that it is possible that coefficients will be found to be significantly different from zero when in fact they are not. The effect of negative autocorrelation is overestimation of the standard error of the estimated coefficient, s_b, which increases the likelihood that coefficients will not be found to be significantly different from zero when indeed they are.

While simply looking at the residual terms may provide some clue to the existence of autocorrelation, many authors report a test statistic called the *Durbin-Watson coefficient*, especially when time series data are being analyzed. This coefficient can be used to test the null hypothesis that successive error terms are not autocorrelated.

When autocorrelation is detected, there are special techniques available to circumvent the problem. Many analysts accept the OLS estimates of the coefficients since they are unbiased but run other statistical procedures to obtain unbiased estimates of the standard errors and t ratios.[5] Some analysts use a technique called *generalized least squares* (GLS) regression to overcome the problem of autocorrelation. This method is based on OLS regression techniques but uses variables that have been transformed.

Heteroskedasticity

Heteroskedasticity refers to another nonrandom pattern in the residual error term. Assumption 3 is that the variability in the error term does not depend on any variable included in the analysis. This assumption is known as the assumption of *homoskedastic errors*; when it is violated, heteroskedasticity is said to exist. The problem arises most frequently in the analysis of cross-sectional data.

---

[5]The most common procedure used is Newey-West.

Consider the relationship between the amount families spend on annual trips to the beach and annual family income. We would expect for families with relatively small incomes that the difference between the amount predicted versus actually spent will be relatively small. But for families with significantly larger incomes the range of residual errors is likely to be greater, in part because the amount they spend going to the beach depends on other things besides income. Thus, we would expect the absolute values of the residual errors in the predicted amount spent going to the beach to be correlated with income. In this case, the residuals are said to be *heteroskedastic.*

As with autocorrelation, heteroskedasticity affects the size of the standard error of the regression coefficient, thereby biasing hypothesis testing results. It does not affect the estimates of the coefficients. The effect on s_b will depend on the exact manner in which the heteroskedasticity was formed. Several different tests are available for detecting the problem of heteroskedasticity. All depend on an examination of the residuals. When the problem is detected, analysts follow the same type of strategy that they follow for autocorrelation. They either accept the OLS estimates of the coefficients and run other procedures to obtain estimates of s_b, or they use GLS to give differential weights to the observations and thereby circumvent the effects of heteroskedasticity on tests of hypothesis.[6]

Additional Topics

Endogeneity and Simultaneous Equations

Even though we warned that causality is never proven by regression analysis, when a researcher specifies that $Y = f(X)$, an implicit causal linkage is frequently assumed. In general, this functional relationship runs from X to Y (i.e., the value of Y is dependent on the value of X). But in many situations the dependency may run both ways (i.e., X is also a function of Y).

One common example of a simultaneous process occurs in the area of criminology. Those cities with higher crime rates are likely to put more resources into crime fighting: *Police = f(Crime)*. At the same time, if police protection is effective, the crime rate should decrease: *Crime = f(Police)*. One could estimate either regression, but in both cases simple linear regression will yield biased estimates of the phenomenon under investigation. This is known as the general problem of endogeneity, and it violates the assumption that the error term is not correlated with any of the assumed independent variables.

The solution to simultaneity is complex and well beyond the scope of this book. It is worthwhile, however, to consider briefly two primary issues that

---

[6]The most common procedures are White and Newey-West. For a discussion of heteroskedasticity, see Kaufman (2013).

are commonly mentioned by analysts investigating simultaneous phenomena: identification and estimation.

Although a variety of methods for estimating simultaneous relationships are available, these techniques require that the coefficients of the model be mathematically obtainable or *identifiable.* Consider the case of the price and quantity of wheat sold each year. Economic theory holds that market prices and quantities are determined by the simultaneous actions of suppliers and demanders. One could easily obtain data on the total wheat marketed each year in the United States and the annual price of wheat for the last several decades. One might then estimate the equation, *Quantity* $= \alpha + \beta$ *Price.* While one would obtain estimates of the parameters, there is no way of knowing or identifying whether the estimated relationship is the demand or the supply relationship, since quantity and price are involved in both relationships.

In order for identification to be possible in such a case, the model must be expanded in some manner. For example, one might argue that quantity demanded (Q_D) is a function of price (P), income (I), and the US population (Pop), while quantity supplied (Q_S) is a function of price and rainfall $(Rain)$. The income, population, and rainfall variables are assumed to be determined outside this market and are called *exogenous variables*, whereas price and quantity (supplied and demanded) are determined within the model and are termed *endogenous variables.* This would yield the following simultaneous equation model, in which the coefficients are identifiable:

$$Q_D = \alpha_1 + \beta_1 P + \beta_2 I + \beta_3 Pop \qquad [5.1]$$

$$Q_S = \alpha_2 + \beta_4 P + \beta_5 Rain \qquad [5.2]$$

This model of a market is said to be *identified,* since unique estimates can be obtained for all seven of the parameters in the model: α_1, α_2, β_1, β_2, β_3, β_4, and β_5. In this instance the coefficients are identifiable since it is possible to solve the system of equations such that each of the two endogenous variables (P and Q) can be expressed as solely a function of the exogenous variables.

A variety of techniques are available to investigators when models are identifiable, although OLS estimation techniques cannot be directly used to estimate the parameters shown in equations 5.1 and 5.2. One commonly used method is called *two-stage least squares,* a technique highly regarded because of its simplicity, ease of computation, and fairly desirable statistical properties. Other estimation techniques include *three-stage least squares* and *maximum likelihood* methods. Advanced study of statistics is required, however, for an understanding of these techniques. Nevertheless, the methods are applied in a variety of circumstances, including estimation of multiple equation macroeconomic models, which are used to forecast the course of the economy.

Experiments

Simple linear regression does not imply causation, as we have stressed repeatedly. But there are situations in which causation can be inferred. One type of situation in which it may be possible to infer causality is if experimental data are available to the analyst. For example, clinical trials to test the effectiveness of a drug randomly divide subjects into two test groups: those who get the treatment and those who do not, but instead get a placebo. After collecting clinical trial data from subjects, it is then common to estimate a linear regression in which some measure of the outcome, such as the number of months survived post treatment, is regressed on a dummy variable that takes the value of 1 for those treated and a value of 0 for those who received the placebo. Because all other variables (such as degree of illness) are assumed to be the same for the two groups due to the randomness of the assignment, the researcher feels reasonably confident that the treatment variable measures a causal effect. Thus, if the coefficient on the variable is found to be significantly different from zero, the researcher has reasonable confidence that treatment caused the better health outcome.[7]

It is far harder for social scientists to conduct experiments, in part because of ethical issues surrounding participation, although occasionally situations present themselves where they can be conducted. For example, there have been experiments in education where students are randomly assigned to a treatment group and a control group. Because of difficulties that can be encountered in conducting experiments, social scientists often look for what can be thought of as "natural" experiments to examine causality. The study of the effect of copyright laws on opera compositions in Italy in the early 19th century provided in Example 4.2 is such an instance. Here the "natural" experiment was the invasion by Napoleon of northern Italy and the imposition, after victory, of French law in the conquered lands. The event qualifies as a natural experiment because composers, at least initially, did not choose to locate there or publish there because of Napoleon's victory. Instead, Napoleon's victory was imposed on them; the imposition of the law is said to be exogenous, that is, outside their control. As a result, characteristics of those who were "treated" by Napoleon's victory were not correlated with ability to write opera, and it is reasonable to make an inference of the causal effect that copyright law had on productivity of composers.

A situation somewhat similar to a natural experiment arises when some criterion is used to determine who is eligible for a treatment. For example,

---

[7]While controlled random experiments are ideal in principle, things can happen that corrupt the experiment. For example, subjects can drop out of the experiment, members of the control group may inadvertently get treated, and some subjects scheduled for treatment may not actually get the treatment.

many states have merit-based scholarship programs in which a student with a GPA of 3.0 or higher gets a scholarship, while others do not. Researchers are interested in knowing whether receipt of the scholarship (the "treatment" in this case) is associated with some positive outcome, such as the probability of graduating. The problem in conducting the analysis is that receipt of a scholarship is correlated with other variables, such as ability, that also might affect the outcome. While GPAs are not randomly assigned to students, one can argue that students with GPAs just above and just below 3.0 are very similar; in particular they have similar ability, and thus the assignment of scholarships to students with a GPA of 3.0 or higher essentially constitutes random assignment to the treated group among students with GPAs slightly above or slightly below 3.0. Researchers make use of this by comparing outcomes of student with GPAs just below 3.0 who did not get the scholarship to those with GPAs just above 3.0 who did. This technique is called *regression discontinuity design.*

Another approach to inferring causality is to compare outcomes for a sample pre- and post-treatment. For example, one might consider the effect of a merit-based scholarship program by comparing student outcomes before the program is adopted to outcomes after the program has been implemented. But is it possible that other things changed that might have affected the outcome of interest. To account for that, one compares the change in outcome for students in the state that adopted a scholarship program to the change in outcome for students in states that did not adopt a scholarship program. Making such a comparison controls for changes that affect all students regardless of the state in which they live. This technique is called *difference-in-differences.* Of course the technique does not control for other changes in the state that adopted the scholarship program that might affect the outcome being considered.

Instrumental Variables

Natural experiments are often not readily available, and in their absence researchers often look for what is called an *instrumental variable*, that is a variable that is correlated with the independent variable but not correlated with the error term. Consider, for example, the study of the productivity of immigrant scientists. A question that policy makers wish to address is whether immigrants are more productive than nonimmigrants. The problem is that immigrants likely are self-selected, in the sense that more able individuals may be more likely to benefit from migration. Since ability is also positively related with productivity, there is a problem of determining causality if one only estimates a model that controls for migration and not ability, which is extremely difficult to measure. One way to address this problem is to identify an "instrument" to estimate the probability of migration that is not correlated with (immeasurable) ability. In a recent paper, Franzoni, Scellato, and Stephan (2014) do precisely this, instrumenting adult migration with the variable "moved when a child." The authors' argument is that the experience of child mobility makes one more open to being mobile but is not related to natural ability.[8] The challenge encountered in using instrumental variables is finding a variable that is correlated with the dependent variable but not the error term, especially when looking for an instrument that makes intuitive sense to the reader.

Limited Dependent Variables

Analysts often wish to study behavior that is observed only as a binary indicator. Examples include whether or not a person is in the labor force, whether or not an applicant was admitted to a university, and whether or not an otherwise qualified voter is registered to vote.

In Chapter 4 we reviewed the use of 0-1 dummy variables as independent variables in regression analysis. While such dichotomous indicators are appropriate as explanatory variables, OLS regression analysis is not appropriate when a 0-1 or another limited choice variable is the dependent variable.

Several problems arise in the case of a 0-1 dependent variable that make the OLS regression inappropriate. Consider the simple case of a model that specifies that individuals with higher income have a greater probability to be registered as Republican voters. The dependent variable, *Republican*, in the model would then be equal to 1 if the person were registered as a Republican and 0 if not (i.e., registered as a Democrat or some other party or not registered). One might estimate the equation, *Republican* = $\alpha + \beta I$, using least squares regression analysis, where I denotes income. A plot of the observations associated with estimating the equation would show some on the horizontal X-axis (representing individuals who did not register as a Republican and hence have a value of Y of zero) at the level of income reported by that individual. Other observations would be shown at the vertical level equal to 1 on the graph and again, the level of I reported by the respondent. You might try to sketch such a two-dimensional graph showing I on the horizontal axis and the 0-1 variable *Republican* on the vertical axis.

While the techniques of Chapter 1 would yield estimates of α and β, several problems can arise. First, it is possible that for certain values of I (together with the estimated a and b) the predicted value of *Republican* would be either less than 0 or greater than 1. But since the predicted value of Republican, $\widehat{Republican}$, can be interpreted as the probability of being a

---

[8]The procedure, which is beyond the scope of this book, uses the instrument (or instruments) to predict the questionable variable and then substitutes this prediction into the regression equation.

Republican, such values do not make sense.[9] Second, the variability of residuals obtained from such an estimation will depend on the size of the independent variable, suggesting that heteroskedasticity is a problem. Finally, while we have not stressed it, the theory that underlies the hypothesis-testing procedure is based on the assumption of normally distributed residuals, which certainly is not the case in this instance.

While OLS regression is theoretically inappropriate in such instances, non-linear estimation techniques have been developed to overcome the major statistical difficulties outlined above. The two techniques most commonly used in such instances are *probit analysis* and *logit analysis.* A study that examines whether foreign-born scientists train in the United States versus elsewhere, for example, is estimated using probit analysis (Stephan, Franzoni, and Scellato, 2015). The primary theoretical difference between probit and logit concerns the probability distributions that underlie the process being analyzed. Nevertheless, each is capable (after some manipulation of the results) of providing estimates of the effect of unit changes in the independent variable(s) on the probability of an event. Moreover, some studies have shown that there is not a great deal of difference in the results obtained using these techniques and the results obtained from an OLS model. However, the OLS model cannot directly yield predictions that will necessarily conform to the laws of probability and still address the issues discussed above.

Models, such as *multinomial logit*, also exist that allow for the analysis of situations in which there are a small number of mutually exclusive outcomes in a choice process (e.g., choice among three types of colleges). In addition, some analysts have used another special technique, termed *Tobit analysis,* when faced with a situation in which many participants in a choice process choose a zero outcome while others choose some positive number that is unlimited in size. An example of such a case is the amount of money a family spends on new car purchases in one year. Many families buy no new car at all ($Y = 0$), while others make purchases anywhere in the range from, say, $15,000 to $65,000.

For completeness, we should also mention that sometimes the dependent variable of interest is limited to nonnegative *counts* of outcomes that are integers. Examples of count variables include the number of home runs, number of patents, and number of tornadoes in any year. OLS is inappropriate when the dependent variable is a count of a positive integer, because it can predict "nonsense" estimates such as a negative number of home runs or fractional number of tornados. In such instances, analysts rely on more sophisticated estimating techniques that take advantage of the fact that the errors in count data are not normally distributed. The two most common

---

[9]A similar problem arises when the value of the dependent variable is restricted to some range, for example percentages that can range from 0 to 100.

techniques for analyzing count data are *Poisson regression* models and *negative binomial regression* models.

Finally, there are also instances when researchers use more complex statistical techniques to analyze a dependent variable that has a limited number of possible outcomes that correspond to some numerical scale. An example of such a variable would be a Likert-scaled outcome with only five or seven possible values. For example, rather than simply measuring whether or not a voter is registered as Republican, a survey may measure on a scale from one to four whether he or she is strongly opposed to a Republican candidate to strongly in support of a Republican candidate. In these cases *ordered probit* or *ordered logit* analytical techniques are generally used.

Conclusions

Linear regression provides a powerful method for analyzing a wide variety of situations. At the same time, this technique relies on a set of assumptions that may or may not hold in different applications. It is our hope that this book will provide the reader an overview of the procedure and a guide to the pitfalls that can befall an analyst who does not pay attention to the assumptions that underlie the technique. Readers who wish to use the procedure themselves are strongly encouraged to consult more advanced books. Examples of such books by topic are given in Appendix D.

APPENDIX A: DERIVATION OF a AND b

The purpose of this appendix is to show how to obtain the values of a and b that minimize the sum of squared error term SSE. From Chapter 1, the sum of the squared errors is given by

$$SSE = \sum(C_i - a - bI_i)^2 \qquad \text{[A1]}$$

where Σ implies summation from $i = 1$ to n. The values of a and b that minimize equation A1 are found by taking the partial derivative of SSE with respect to a and b and setting the resulting derivatives equal to zero. This yields

$$\partial SSE/_{\partial a} = (-2)\sum(C_i - a - bI_i) = 0 \qquad \text{[A2]}$$

$$\partial SSE/_{\partial b} = (-2)\sum\left[(I_i)(C_i - a - bI_i)\right] = 0 \qquad \text{[A3]}$$

Dividing through both A2 and A3 by -2 and rearranging terms yields

$$\sum C_i = an + b\sum I_i \qquad \text{[A4]}$$

$$\sum(C_iI_i) = a\sum I_i + b\sum(I_i^2) \qquad \text{[A5]}$$

where $\Sigma a = an$ and n is the sample size.

Equations A4 and A5 are in the standard form of the normal equations for a straight line. The terms $\sum C_i$, $\sum I_i$, $\sum C_iI_i$, and $\sum I_i^2$ can be computed from the data set. Equations A4 and A5 can then be solved simultaneously for a and b. The resulting values of a and b minimize SSE.

Equations A4 and A5 can also be solved to obtain formulas for the values of a and b. The formula for b is

$$b = \sum[(I_i - \bar{I})(C_i - \bar{C})] / \sum(I_i - \bar{I})^2 \qquad \text{[A6]}$$

where $\bar{C}$ and $\bar{I}$ represent the means of C and I, respectively.

Once b is known, a can be obtained by using the expression

$$\bar{C} = a + b\bar{I} \qquad \text{[A7]}$$

which is obtained by dividing equation A4 by n. The derivation of equation A6 is tedious but not difficult and is presented in most statistics books.

Notice that equation A7 says that the regression line passes through the point defined by the mean values of C and I.

Equations A4 and A5 can be used to obtain estimates of a and b for the food consumption problem. From the data in Table 1, the following values can be obtained:

$$\Sigma C_i = 439,757$$

$$\Sigma I_i = 3,616,086$$

$$\Sigma C_i I_i = 41,028,608,253$$

$$\Sigma I_i^2 = 405,304,167,128$$

$$n = 50$$

Substituting these values into equations A4 and A5 yields

$$439,757 = a(50) + b(3,616,086) \qquad\qquad \text{[A4']}$$

$$41,028,608,253 = 3,616,086 + b(405,028,608,253) \qquad \text{[A5']}$$

These two equations are then solved simultaneously to yield $a = 4155.21$ and $b = 0.064$.

APPENDIX B: CRITICAL VALUES FOR STUDENT'S t DISTRIBUTION

Level of Significance (percentage) Values for Right-Tail Test[1]

Degrees of Freedom	10%	5%	2.5%	1%	.5%
1	3.0777	6.3138	12.7062	31.8207	63.6574
2	1.8856	2.9200	4.3027	6.9646	9.9248
3	1.6377	2.3534	3.1824	4.5407	5.8409
4	1.5332	2.1318	2.7764	3.7469	4.6041
5	1.4759	2.0150	2.5706	3.3649	4.0322
6	1.4398	1.9432	2.4469	3.1427	3.7074
7	1.4149	1.8946	2.3646	2.9980	3.4995
8	1.3968	1.8595	2.3060	2.8965	3.3554
9	1.3830	1.8331	2.2622	2.8214	3.2498
10	1.3722	1.8125	2.2281	2.7638	3.1693
11	1.3634	1.7959	2.2010	2.7181	3.1058
12	1.3562	1.7823	2.1788	2.6810	3.0545
13	1.3502	1.7709	2.1604	2.6503	3.0123
14	1.3450	1.7613	2.1448	2.6245	2.9768
15	1.3406	1.7531	2.1315	2.6025	2.9467
16	1.3368	1.7459	2.1199	2.5835	2.9208
17	1.3334	1.7396	2.1098	2.5669	2.8982
18	1.3304	1.7341	2.1009	2.5524	2.8784
19	1.3277	1.7291	2.0930	2.5395	2.8609
20	1.3253	1.7247	2.0860	2.5280	2.8453
21	1.3232	1.7207	2.0796	2.5177	2.8314
22	1.3212	1.7171	2.0739	2.5083	2.8188
23	1.3195	1.7139	2.0687	2.4999	2.8073
24	1.3178	1.7109	2.0639	2.4922	2.7969
25	1.3163	1.7081	2.0595	2.4851	2.7874

(Continued)

---

[1] For a left-tail test the appropriate t statistic will be negative. Thus, for 10 degrees of freedom and at the 1% level of significance, the t statistic is −2.7638. For a two-tail test the level of significance must be doubled. This implies, for example, that with 50 degrees of freedom the t statistic of 1.6759 is associated with a significance level of 10%, not 5%.

88

(Continued)

Degrees of Freedom	10%	5%	2.5%	1%	.5%
26	1.3150	1.7056	2.0555	2.4786	2.7787
27	1.3137	1.7033	2.0518	2.4727	2.7707
28	1.3125	1.7011	2.0484	2.4671	2.7633
29	1.3114	1.6991	2.0452	2.4620	2.7564
30	1.3104	1.6973	2.0423	2.4573	2.7500
31	1.3095	1.6955	2.0395	2.4528	2.7440
32	1.3086	1.6939	2.0369	2.4487	2.7385
33	1.3077	1.6924	2.0345	2.4448	2.7333
34	1.3070	1.6909	2.0322	2.4411	2.7284
35	1.3062	1.6896	2.0301	2.4377	2.7238
36	1.3055	1.6883	2.0281	2.4345	2.7195
37	1.3049	1.6871	2.0262	2.4314	2.7154
38	1.3042	1.6860	2.0244	2.4286	2.7116
39	1.3036	1.6849	2.0227	2.4258	2.7079
40	1.3031	1.6839	2.0211	2.4233	2.7045
41	1.3025	1.6829	2.0195	2.4208	2.7012
42	1.3020	1.6820	2.0181	2.4185	2.6981
43	1.3016	1.6811	2.0167	2.4163	2.6951
44	1.3011	1.6802	2.0154	2.4141	2.6923
45	1.3006	1.6794	2.0141	2.4121	2.6896
46	1.3002	1.6787	2.0129	2.4102	2.6870
47	1.2998	1.6779	2.0117	2.4083	2.6846
48	1.2994	1.6772	2.0106	2.4066	2.6822
49	1.2991	1.6766	2.0096	2.4049	2.6800
50	1.2987	1.6759	2.0086	2.4033	2.6778
60	1.2958	1.6706	2.0003	2.3901	2.6603
70	1.2938	1.6669	1.9944	2.3808	2.6479
80	1.2922	1.6641	1.9901	2.3739	2.6387
90	1.2910	1.6620	1.9867	2.3685	2.6316
∞	1.2816	1.6449	1.9600	2.3263	2.5758

Source: Owen (1962), courtesy Atomic Energy Commission, Washington, DC.

APPENDIX C: REGRESSION OUTPUT FROM SAS, STATA, SPSS, R, AND EXCEL

Regression programs in use in most universities and research centers in 2016 are part of the SAS® (Statistical Analysis System), Stata®, IBM® SPSS® (Statistical Package for the Social Sciences), and R statistical packages.[1] (Statistical packages are designed specifically to carry out a wide variety of statistical analyses beyond multiple regression analysis.) In addition, the Excel® spreadsheet program can be used to conduct some statistical procedures.

The purpose of this appendix is to illustrate where, on the outputs from these various programs, you can find the statistics that are discussed in the text. To facilitate the discussion, we have used the same data shown in Table 1.1 to estimate the regression equation 2.1.

Parameter estimates, standard errors, t ratios, and p-values: All of the programs show the estimated regression coefficients and their associated standard errors along with the t ratios that can be used to test the null hypothesis that the regression coefficient is equal to zero. In addition, each show the prob-value associated with a two-tail test of that null hypothesis.

There are some differences in specific terms used in the different programs. For example, SAS, Stata, and R use the term $Pr > |t|$ to denote the prob-value, whereas Excel uses p-value, and SPSS uses "Sig" to denote the level of significance. Also, some of the programs use the term *intercept* whereas others use the term *constant* to refer to the estimate of the parameter α as shown in equation 2.1.[2]

Stata and Excel go further and also show 95% confidence intervals constructed around the estimated regression coefficients. SPSS also shows the estimated beta coefficient discussed in Chapter 2.[3]

Associated Statistics: Each of the programs computes and displays both the R^2 and adjusted R^2 ($\bar{R}^2$), with SPSS and Excel also displaying

---

SPSS is a registered trademark of IBM Corporation. SAS is a registered trademark of the SAS Institute, Inc. Stata is a registered trademark of StataCorp LP. Microsoft, Excel, and Windows are either registered trademarks or trademarks of Microsoft Corporation in the United States and/or other countries.

[1] We acknowledge that these are not the only programs available; however, they are among the most commonly used.

[2] Note that values may be expressed in scientific notation. For example, Excel reports the p-value for I as 8.6E-08, which means that the decimal place is eight places to the left of the 8 (note the negative sign on 08), i.e., 0.000000086. R uses a lowercase e rather than an uppercase E.

[3] The discussion here is based on the standard outputs from these programs; most also have other optional statistics that can be computed, including, for example, the Durbin Watson statistic discussed in Chapter 5.

the multiple correlation coefficient R. The F statistic used to test the null hypothesis $H_0: \beta_1 = \beta_2 = 0$ is also shown along with the degrees of freedom (*df*) and level of significance associated with that hypothesis.

Each of the programs' outputs, except for that of the R program, allow you to verify the computed value of the coefficient of determination. If you divide the sum of squares for the model (denoted "regression" in both SPSS and Excel) by the total sum of squares, the result will be equal to the R^2. This is equivalent to what is calculated using equation 1.10.

One other statistic mentioned in Chapter 1 is the sum of the squared errors. This is also found in the outputs from each of the programs other than R. In each it is shown in the column headed Sum of Squares; in SAS it's in the "Error" row, whereas in the other programs it is called the "Residual."

SAS

The SAS System

The REG Procedure
Model: MODEL1
Dependent Variable: C Food Consumption

Number of Observations Read   50

Number of Observations Used   50

Analysis of Variance

Source	DF	Sum of Squares	Mean Square	F Value	Pr > F
Model	2	640141353	320070676	37.98	<.0001
Error	47	396033619	8426247		
Corrected Total	49	1036174972			

Root MSE	2902.79989	R-Square	0.6178
Dependent Mean	8795.14000	Adj R-Sq	0.6015
Coeff Var	33.00459		

Parameter Estimates

Variable	Label	DF	Parameter Estimate	Standard Error	t Value	Pr > |t|
Intercept	Intercept	1	2962.94861	850.25843	3.48	0.0011
I	Income	1	0.05461	0.00863	6.33	<.0001
S	Family Size	1	825.77886	344.84230	2.39	0.0207

92

Stata

Statistics/Data Analysis

Source	SS	df	MS			
				Number of obs	=	50
				F(2, 47)	=	37.98
Model	640141353	2	320070676	Prob > F	=	0.0000
Residual	396033619	47	8426247.21	R-squared	=	0.6178
				Adj R-squared	=	0.6015
Total	1.0362e+09	49	21146428	Root MSE	=	2902.8

C	Coef.	Std. Err.	t	P>|t|	[95% Conf. Interval]	
I	.054609	.0086314	6.33	0.000	.0372448	.0719731
S	825.7789	344.8423	2.39	0.021	132.0456	1519.512
_cons	2962.949	850.2584	3.48	0.001	1252.449	4673.448

SPSS

Variables Entered/Removed[a]

Model	Variables Entered	Variables Removed	Method
1	S, I[b]	.	Enter

a. Dependent Variable: C
b. All requested variables entered.

Model Summary

Model	R	R Square	Adjusted R Square	Std. Error of the Estimate
1	.786[a]	.618	.602	2902.800

a. Predictors: (Constant), S, I

ANOVA[a]

Model		Sum of Squares	df	Mean Square	F	Sig.
1	Regression	640141352.981	2	320070676.491	37.985	.000[b]
	Residual	396033619.039	47	8426247.214		
	Total	1036174972.020	49			

a. Dependent Variable: C
b. Predictors: (Constant), S, I

Coefficients[a]

Model		Unstandardized Coefficients		Standardized Coefficients	t	Sig.
		B	Std. Error	Beta		
1	(Constant)	2962.949	850.258		3.485	.001
	I	.055	.009	.643	6.327	.000
	S	825.779	344.842	.243	2.395	.021

a. Dependent Variable: C

R

```
Residuals:
    Min      1Q  Median      3Q     Max
-4793.2 -1678.5  -128.3  1376.2  7379.1

Coefficients:
             Estimate Std. Error t value Pr(>|t|)
(Intercept) 2.963e+03  8.503e+02   3.485  0.00108 **
Income      5.461e-02  8.631e-03   6.327  8.6e-08 ***
Family.Size 8.258e+02  3.448e+02   2.395  0.02068 *
---
Signif. codes:  0 '***' 0.001 '**' 0.01 '*' 0.05 '.' 0.1 ' ' 1

Residual standard error: 2903 on 47 degrees of freedom
Multiple R-squared:  0.6178,    Adjusted R-squared:  0.6015
F-statistic: 37.98 on 2 and 47 DF,  p-value: 1.528e-10
```

Microsoft EXCEL

Regression Statistics

Multiple R	0.785998
R Square	0.617793
Adjusted R Square	0.601529
Standard Error	2902.8
Observations	50

ANOVA

	df	SS	MS	F	Significance F
Regression	2	640141353	320070676	37.98496	1.52766E-10
Residual	47	396033619	842624721		
Total	49	1036174972			

	Coefficients	Standard Error	t Stat	P-value	Lower 95%	Upper 95%
Intercept	2962.949	850.2584316	3.4847624	0.001077	1252.44928	4673.447948
Income	0.054609	0.008631406	6.32677727	8.6E-08	0.037244834	0.071973132
Family Size	825.7789	344.8423009	2.3946565	0.020675	132.0456285	1519.512083

APPENDIX D: SUGGESTED TEXTBOOKS

A large number of textbooks focus to some extent on linear regression analysis. Most introductory statistics texts devote at least one chapter to the subject, while econometrics textbooks tend to focus nearly exclusively on linear regression. Among the potential books in these areas are the following:

Introductory Statistics

Larson, Ron, and Elizabeth Farber. 2015. *Elementary Statistics: Picturing the World.* 6th ed. Boston: Pearson.

Meier, Kenneth J., Jeffrey L. Brudney, and John Bohta. 2015. *Applied Statistics for Public and Nonprofit Administration.* 9th ed. Stamford, CT: Cengage Learning.

Moore, David, George P. McCabe, Layth C. Alwan, and Bruce A. Craig. 2016. *The Practice of Statistics for Business and Economics.* 4th ed. New York: Macmillan Learning.

Stine, Robert A., and Dean P. Foster. 2014. *Statistics for Business: Decision Making and Analysis.* 2nd ed. Boston: Pearson.

There are also introductory textbooks for statistics designed for specific disciplines such as political science, sociology, or education.

Regression-Oriented Texts

Fox, John. 2015. *Applied Regression Analysis & Generalized Linear Models.* 3rd ed. Thousand Oaks, CA: Sage.

Mendenhall, William, and Terry A. Sincich. 2011. *A Second Course in Statistics: Regression Analysis.* 7th ed. Boston: Pearson.

Montgomery, Douglas C. 2013. *Introduction to Linear Regression Analysis.* 5th ed. Hoboken, NJ: Wiley.

Weisberg, Sanford. 2013. *Applied Linear Regression.* 4th ed. Hoboken, NJ: Wiley.

In addition, many of the books in this Sage series, Quantitative Applications in the Social Sciences, focus on linear regression topics.

Econometrics

Bailey, Michael A. 2015. *Real Stats: Using Econometrics for Political Science and Public Policy.* New York: Oxford University Press.

Gujarati, Damodar, and Dawn Porter. 2010. *Essentials of Econometrics.* 4th ed. New York: McGraw-Hill/Irwin.

Hill, R. Carter, William E. Griffiths, and Guay C. Lim. 2011. *Principles of Econometrics.* 4th ed. Hoboken, NJ: Wiley.

Stock, James H., and Mark W. Watson. 2011. *Introduction to Econometrics.* 3rd ed. Boston: Addison-Wesley.

Wooldridge, Jeffrey M. 2013. *Introductory Econometrics: A Modern Approach.* 5th ed. Mason, OH: South-Western Cengage Learning.

REFERENCES

Arzaghi, Mohammad, and Jay Squalli. 2015. "How Price Inelastic Is Demand for Gasoline in Fuel-Subsidizing Economies?" *Energy Economics* 50: 117–124.

Cavazos-Rehg, Patricia A., Melissa J. Krauss, Edward L. Spitznagel, Frank J. Chaloupka, Douglas A. Luke, Brian Waterman, Richard A. Grucza, and Laura Jean Bierut. 2014. "Differential Effects of Cigarette Price Changes on Adult Smoking Behavior." *Tobacco Control* 232: 113–118.

Chandra, Ambarish, Sumeet Gulati, and Milind Kandlikar. 2010. "Green Drivers or Free Riders? An Analysis of Tax Rebates for Hybrid Vehicles." *Journal of Environmental Economics and Management* 602: 78–93.

Currie, Janet, Stefano Della Vigne, Enrico Moretti, and Vikram Pathania. 2010. "The Effect of Fast Food Restaurants on Obesity and Weight." *American Economic Journal: Economic Policy* 2: 32–63.

Dahl, Gordon, and Stefano Della Vigne. 2009. "Does Movie Violence Increase Violent Crime?" *Quarterly Journal of Economics* 124: 677–734.

Franzoni, Chiara, Giuseppe Scellato, and Paula Stephan. 2014. "Mobile Scientists: Superior Performance of Migrant Scientists." *Economics Letters* 122: 89–93.

Giorcelli, Michela, and Petra Moser. 2015. "Copyright and Creativity: Evidence From Italian Operas." Accessed November 25. http://papers.ssrn.com/sol3/Papers.cfm?abstract_id=2505776.

Givati, Yehonatan, and Ugo Troiano. 2012. "Law, Economics, and Culture: Theory of Mandated Benefits and Evidence From Maternity Leave Policies." *Journal of Law and Economics* 55 (May): 339–364.

Goldin, Claudia, and Lawrence F. Katz. 2008. *The Race Between Education and Technology.* Cambridge, MA: Belknap Press of Harvard University Press.

Goolsbee, Austan D., and Alan B. Krueger. 2015. "A Retrospective Look at Rescuing and Restructuring General Motors and Chrysler" *The Journal of Economic Perspectives* 29 (2): 3–23.

Hajnal, Zoltan, and Michael U. Rivera. 2014. "Immigration, Latinos, and White Partisan Politics: The New Democratic Defection." *American Journal of Political Science* 58 (4): 773–789.

Hall, Joshua C., and Chris Shultz. 2015. "Determinants of Voting Behaviour on the Keystone XL Pipeline." *Applied Economic Letters.* 01 September 2015. http://www.tandfonline.com/doi/abs/10.1080/13504851.2015.1083077

Hanlon, W. Walker, and Yuan Tian. 2015. "Killer Cities: Past and Present." *American Economic Review: Papers & Proceedings* 105 (5): 570–575.

Hardy, Melissa A. 1993. *Regression With Dummy Variables.* Thousand Oaks, CA: Sage.

Kaufman, Robert L. 2013. *Heteroskedasticity in Regression: Detection and Correction.* Thousand Oaks, CA: Sage.

Krishan, Kewal, Tanuj Kanchan, and Abhilasha Sharma. 2012. "Multiplication Factor Versus Regression Analysis in Stature Estimation From Hand and Foot Dimensions." *Journal of Forensic and Legal Medicine* 19: 211–214.

Landes, William M., and Sonia Lahr-Pastor. 2011. "Measuring Coase's Influence." *Journal of Law and Economics* 544: S383–S401.

Linder, Andrew, Melissa Lindquist, and Julie Arnold. 2015. "Million Dollar Maybe? The Effect of Female Presence in Movies on Box Office Returns." *Sociological Inquiry* 853: 407–428.

McCloskey, D. M. 1985. "The Loss Function Has Been Mislaid: The Rhetoric of Significance Tests." *American Economic Review* 75: 201–205.

Oster, Emily. 2004. "Witchcraft, Weather and Economic Growth in Renaissance Europe." *Journal of Economic Perspectives* 18 (1): 215–228.

Rotolo, Thomas, John Wilson, and Nathan Dietz. 2015. "Volunteering in the United States in the Aftermath of the Foreclosure Crisis." *Nonprofit and Voluntary Sector Quarterly* 44 (5): 924–944.

Spera, Christopher, Robin Ghertner, Anthony Nerino, and Adrienne DiTommaso. 2015. "Out of Work? Volunteers Have Higher Odds of Getting Back to Work." *Nonprofit and Voluntary Sector Quarterly* 44 (5): 886–907.

Stephan, Paula, Chiara Franzoni, and Giuseppe Scellato. 2015. "Global Competition for Scientific Talent: Evidence From Location Decisions of PhDs and Postdocs in 16 Countries." *Industrial and Corporate Change.* doi:10.1093/icc/dtv037

Wiemers, Emily. 2014. "The Effect of Unemployment on Household Composition and Doubling Up." *Demography* 51 (6): 2155–2178.

INDEX